Beneath
the Surface

Beneath
the Surface

by ANDREW TEAGUE McCOLLISTER

Editor
Carolyn Bredschneider

Senior Publisher
Steven Lawrence Hill Sr

ASA Publishing Corporation

A Publisher Trademark Title page

ASA Publishing Corporation
An Accredited Publishing House with the BBB
www.asapublishingcorporation.com

The Landmark Building
23 E. Front St., Suite 103, Monroe, Michigan 48161

Copyrights©2018 Andrew Teague McCollister, All Rights Reserved
Book Title: Beneath the Surface
Date Published: 02.26.2018 / Edition 1 *Trade Paperback*
Book ID: ASAPCID2380743
ISBN: 978-1-946746-27-6
Library of Congress Cataloging-in-Publication Data

This book was published in the United States of America.
Great State of Michigan

A Publisher Trademark Copyrights page

Dedication

Dedicated To:

The Best Parents a Child Could Ask For-

Rick McCollister and Kathey Teague-McCollister

And

My Most Loyal Fan and Godmother

Margrit Hopkins

TABLE
OF
CONTENTS

Dedication

Table of Contents

Preface

"How can you be satisfied? I can be pleased, but never satisfied. I'll be satisfied when I'm turning in my grave."

This was my mother's response when Dad suggested we end our two and a half weeks' vacation a day early. He made the mistake of telling Mom he was satisfied with the trip. Though my preference would've been to return home and spend an extra day nestled between my couch cushions watching segmented reruns of *Modern Family* between periodic naps, I had to admit there was some truth to her words.

Can we ever be truly satisfied? A simple question with a highly ambiguous answer. Some people could cure the world of cancer and still want more. Others, including myself, find satisfaction by making it to work without a GPS. Perhaps, it's a matter of perspective.

In school I was never satisfied, least of all in English class. I always liked reading, but despised being tested on it. It seemed strange that I could lose points on a paper asking my opinion of a novel.

"It's because your opinion doesn't match the opinion the author was trying to convey," my teacher said.

I wasn't satisfied with her answer. Her name wasn't printed on the front cover and most of the books we read were published over a hundred years ago. I didn't see how she could possibly know what the author was trying to say. On top of that, I didn't understand why writers had to hide behind symbolism. Was I really expected to believe because the main character stopped to smell a flower, she was secretly regretting cheating on her husband and decided the only way to make herself happy was to kill her lover?

I started writing stories in the eighth grade. My first full length epic was titled *The Four Psychics*. I prided myself on producing a story lacking any symbolism or flowery language. If there was something I wanted the audience to know, I stated it in plain English. The result was about ten pages consisting of a world where the only characters were thirteen-year-old white boys with one-syllable names and everyone announced what was happening around them.

"Oh no," Tom screamed. "He is attacking me with a psychic blast."

"Don't worry," John said as he jumped in front of Tom. "I'll protect you with my psychic shield."

Needless to say, I wasn't satisfied.

In college, I adopted an English major after taking a Creative Writing: Fiction course. The class taught me many fundamentals of writing, one of which was that characters were actually allowed to have differences. This led to my first short story, *The College Experience*.

Following the class, I began writing more often. I rewrote *The Four Psychics*. This time I made one of the psychics a girl, one black, and one almost two years older than the others. Clearly having mastered the diversity of fiction writing, I decided to take Creative Writing: Non-Fiction.

I didn't expect to get much from the class. I was a fiction writer. With fiction I could make the world whatever I wanted. The possibilities were limitless! Why would anyone be satisfied reading about my life, where limitations such as gravity and Newton's laws applied?

However, when I read *Naked* by non-fiction writer David Sedaris, I became captivated by his words. Sure, he never woke up one morning with the ability to leap the tallest building with a single bound, but he did do something that no work of fiction ever did for me. For the first time, I found myself relating not to some imaginary character, but to a real human with blood in his veins and breath in his lungs.

When my mother read *Naked*, I asked her what she thought of David's development of his characters. "I don't read books thinking about character development," she said. "If the author wants me to think something, he'll tell me."

"If he just told you, it would ruin it," I said. "It's an author's job to make their readers think."

With those words, I realized something. Despite my years of challenging symbolism and rejecting poetic language, I'd somehow ended up a writer.

Through the inspiration of Sedaris, I revisited *The College Experience*. With a new perspective, I started writing not what I wanted the characters to do, but instead what **they** would do. This led to the birth of *Beneath the Surface*.

I suppose a question people will want to ask is whether I'm satisfied with *Beneath the Surface*. The answer is no. When I turn on the wrong street, or wake up suddenly from a nap, it's usually with a new idea: another character I should have developed or another scene I should have added.

I don't think I'm meant to ever be completely satisfied with my work. The question becomes, can I satisfy my reader? A simple question, with an ambiguous answer only known by you.

Beneath
the Surface

by ANDREW TEAGUE McCOLLISTER

Bathroom

The bathroom was constructed to fit the morning rituals of my mother. A small television, only capable of the news station, sat facing the cushioned seat and foot warmer. Only one of the two sinks was usable. The one on the right was home to several plastic baggies, each containing the exact same amount of cereal. For a short time, the sink also held a blonde wig fashioned from real human hair. By the door, within reaching distance of the cushioned seat, sat a box of Cheerios. Although my mother never ate Cheerios, she did enjoy treating the family dog.

I can still remember the sound of Arthur's paws clicking against the wooden floor as he scampered to Mom's open bathroom. The ceiling fan blazed over the hum of her foot warmer, on occasion squeaking so loud that it sent the dog running away in fear. No matter what, he always chanced the fan for his Cheerios.

I'm not sure if Mom saw me watching, but if she did she pretended not to. I would poke my head inside her bathroom door and see her head bent down over the sink, watching our dog chew his cereal.

***

After my last summer swim meet, Mom confessed to me that she had been treated for breast cancer. "But it's alright now," she said.

I must have been thirteen. She sat alongside my father in a Cracker Barrel, her pale scalp hidden from view by the blonde wig. I don't remember what I said. I only remember the buttermilk pancakes and grits I ordered.

The normal emotions to feel at a time like this would've been anger, frustration, fear, even sadness. I learned that from the books my father bought. These were the emotions my mother had wanted at Cracker Barrel.

The only thing I felt was disappointment in myself. For a year, I had believed that she missed work three times a month to go shopping. For a year, I didn't ask about the medicine that made her hair fall out. For a year, I believed what she told me. It was nightmares that caused her to wail in pain after dark.

During the year of her treatment, I had even allowed myself to be angry with her for missing my swim meets. Her excuse had been "No one talks to me there. It's boring."

***

Now, though, my mother had her hair back. It came back long and curly thanks to the Rogaine. She even had a blonde beard where the liquid had dripped down her face. With her new hair, she retired from her job and planned an out of country trip for the family every summer. It was as if she needed to see the world.

Looking back, I wish I had cried over her news or even faked a few fights with her to show that I did care. We only had one fight regarding her cancer, and it was years later, after the cancer was past and the beard had been trimmed.

I'd wrapped my new car around another at a local intersection. No one had been hurt, but both cars were totaled. The wreck was my fault. My parents paid the bill and we returned home.

Later that week, I came home from swim practice

tired, grumpy, and with three unfinished homework projects. Mom asked me to tidy up the den and to put away her dirty dishes. I told her that it was her mess.

"I would think that you would want to help out after all the money your car crash has cost."

"I would think that you would want to help out after all the money your cancer bills cost us," I said, startling myself.

She locked herself in her bathroom. I didn't see her for the rest of the night, but I could hear the screeching ceiling fan sheltering her tears.

Dad asked me later, "Do you even care about what she had to go through?"

"If she had wanted me to worry, then she should have told me when she was sick," I cried after I spoke.

***

Mom later told me that she regretted not taking pictures of her bald head. Pictures would have been a symbol of her pain and accomplishment. They would have allowed her to always remember what she went through and remind her to keep striving to live her life to the fullest.

I don't need a picture of her, though. Anytime I think

about my mother's cancer, I hear the clicking of Arthur's paws darting past me. I see the shadow of his curled tail, the front of his body disappearing in the doorway, flinching at the squeak of the fan.

In the bathroom, I picture my mother's head bent down, her scalp visible through the few wispy hairs that she refused to shave, and her wig in the sink resting comfortably on the Styrofoam head. But I wasn't looking at the wig. I was looking at my mother, smiling, as Arthur licked the cereal out of her hand.

The College Experience

Mallory spread out on her bed. "I don't live with anyone," she said. "It's kind of nice to have a room to myself, but it gets lonely."

"You can probably request a roommate," I said. She was an attractive girl. I knew my mom would like the cross hanging from her neck. Her room was bare, except for a handful of picture frames scattered around her desk. The photos almost appeared to be the same image photoshopped amongst different backgrounds. They all depicted Mallory casually smiling with an elderly woman I assumed to be her grandmother. I noticed they sported matching cross necklaces.

At first, our meeting was purely business. We both needed a study partner for Chemistry, and lived in the same dorm. However, I soon found these 'study sessions' consisted more of stories about her house cat, Ginger, than of periodic elements.

The first few weeks of college life consisted of Mallory and me eating, going to class, and having our 'study dates.' I knew it wouldn't remain that simple. Soon I would plunge into the swim season. That meant double practices at 6:00 AM and 3:00 PM.

Four days before my freedom ended, I found myself on Mallory's bed watching a video of her giving Ginger a bath. While the cat's shriek and frantic scamper to safety behind the toilet was funny, it did trigger a bad thought.

"I think I should swim some laps," I said. Counting my summer vacation, I was approaching six weeks of no practice. I got up to leave, but felt Mallory tug at my arm.

"Not tonight, we'll go tomorrow." She didn't take her eyes off Ginger, who was now being pursued by a blow-dryer.

I told her once practice started I would be on a strict schedule. "Coach only lets us miss one practice a month."

"I understand," she said. She told me her Spanish club

started next month, and they had two meetings a week. "We'll both make time for each other."

The next day, Mallory kept her promise of going to the pool. "I'm a pretty good swimmer. I have a pool in my backyard," she boasted.

It took her twenty minutes to assemble her swim attire. Her two-piece suit came complete with a nose clip, ear plugs, and two sunflowers in place of her nipples. Though I warned her it might get lost, she continued to wear the cross around her neck.

When we entered the pool, the bitter smell of chlorine choked my nostrils. Instantly, beads of hot sweat ran down my bare body. I raised my hand to shield my eyes from the somehow piercing fluorescent lights.

The ceiling was surrounded by the massive coiling vents, breathing out chilled air onto their victims. There were no windows to be seen, only six rusted diving blocks and two sets of creaky bleachers.

I looked around the dungeon where I would spend my college years swimming.

"Why are those ugly ropes in the pool?" Mallory said through her nose piece.

"Those are lane lines. They divide the pool for

practice." She was right about them being ugly. They were chipped and covered with rust, but that was the least of my concerns. I focused on the pool's shallow end and tried to imagine myself finding the courage to plunge into the chemical infested water every morning. Then I noticed short, but steady waves coming from the deeper end.

I expanded my gaze and saw someone moving through the water. He was moving with a fast, constant speed that almost looked effortless. His arms cut through the water like it was no more than air. I had seen fast swimmers before but there was something about his stroke, something about him that just fascinated me.

"Who is that?"

"I don't know. He must be another swimmer."

"He's practicing. We can come back later." She had already turned to leave.

Did she expect us to have the pool to ourselves? "You go ahead," I said. "I'm going to swim."

I didn't look back at Mallory, but assumed she eventually left. I told myself I would only watch this guy a couple more minutes. I don't know how much time passed, but before I knew it the mystery swimmer had come to a stop. He slowly lifted himself from the pool and began to make his way towards me.

He stood tall and lean with long legs and noticeable muscles on his thighs. His chest was equally well defined. My eyes moved to his face. He had bright blue eyes, a small button nose, thin lips, and as he removed his swim cap, I noticed the fine mess of blond hair that accompanied his scalp.

There he stood, a six foot, two inch tall man with water slowly running down his body, with his hand extended. "Hey," he said with a noticeable accent, "I'm Niles Ludren. Are you on the swim team?"

I reasoned he was one of the Swedish recruits I had heard about. I grabbed his hand. He clenched mine in a firm, overpowering handshake. "I'm Conner Mills, and yes, I am."

"Nice," he said. Then he reached down to grab his swimsuit, and began to pull it lower on his body. The fabric clenched tight to his thighs, but once it passed them, the wet suit fell easily down his legs and around his ankles.

I was not prepared to be on a team with a nudist. I imagined that in Sweden, people were more open and comfortable with their bodies, but this was ridiculous. He offered no warning of his stripping. Normally, I would have averted my gaze and found some reason to quickly relocate myself, but just as I had been transfixed by his swimming I found the same effect occurring now.

I followed a solitary drop migrating down his forehead. I couldn't tell if it was pool water or his sweat. The mystery droplet journeyed past his shaved armpits, through his smooth chest, and stopped just short of his uncircumcised penis.

He slowly caressed his body with a white towel. I watched him change into his clothes. His boxers slid up his thighs and concealed him from my gaze. He eased his jeans over his bare legs and finally slid a t-shirt over his body. All the while he had been making small talk with me. What he said, I don't remember. I can only recall responding with words like "yes" and "oh really."

"I'll see you later, Conner," he said.

Then I watched him swing his swim bag over his broad shoulders and casually walk away from the pool with his head held high.

***

My first day of practice was a quiet one. I didn't really know anyone and appeared to be one of the only Americans on the team. The freshman Swedish guys stood with their homeland upperclassmen conversing in something that sounded like chipmunks singing. Meanwhile, a group of mixed Europeans talked loudly about how they "can't believe the American health care system is so shitty."

Niles wasn't the only one who enjoyed showing off his body. All the foreigners wore tight swimsuits that failed to cover all their privates. I felt like an outcast already because my jammer suit covered the majority of my thighs.

"Let's get moving," Coach said.

The team utilized the limited deck space and crowded behind the different lanes. I thought about joining Niles's lane, but it was already overstuffed with accented individuals. *They seemed so old.* Many of the foreigners were significantly taller than me and sported massive amounts of facial hair. I later found out that many Europeans graduated high school later than us. Eventually, I settled into an end lane with some other Americans.

As soon as our coach announced the set, Niles had his goggles and cap mounted. "Let's go boys," he said. He did a cannonball into the water and burst into a sprint. I, along with the rest of the freshman, tightened the pool ropes separating the lanes.

The dungeon water was as humid as expected. I eased out thoughts about the temperature and restricted air quality, and focused on my stroke. *Right arm, left arm, breath, right arm, left arm, flip turn, streamline, right arm, left arm, breath . . .*

After several repeated cycles, I completed the set and rested on the wall. "Good job Conner," Coach said. I looked around the vacant wall and realized I finished practice first.

"Go ahead and hit the showers," Coach said. *That was new*. My high school team always waited for everyone to finish before leaving.

The locker rooms were identical to the pool in terms of size and cleanliness. The showers were side by side in one room with no walls or curtains dividing them. In high school, I would have showered and gone home. Here, I didn't know what the proper procedure was. I spent ten minutes letting the warm water run over me.

I closed my eyes and proceeded with my third attempt to rinse the chlorine from my hair. "What the hell are you doing? That's my shower." I opened my eyes and saw one of the foreigners towering over me. His massive arms were crossed over a blanket of chest hair. I didn't know if he was a freshman or not, but he must have had three years on me.

"I'm sorry. I was just finishing . . ."

"Isn't it first come first serve?" I recognized the accent. Niles entered the shower room. "If you want the good one, you'll have to finish practice faster."

The Viking glared at Niles for a moment, then laughed. "That shower's the shit. I'm going to get it back tomorrow." He lightly punched my shoulder and moved to the shower next to me.

I thought about saying something to Niles, but then the rest of the team poured into the room. Practically in unison, they removed their swimsuits and proceeded to wash their manhood. A few teammates told me I did well in practice. I came close to mentioning how different the practice style was from high school, but found myself unable to say more than a soft "Thanks" and continue staring down at my still-present swimsuit.

Despite my head start, I was the last to leave the shower room. I figured the locker room was still nudist territory. Once I heard the commotion die down and the door slam shut, I reasoned the coast was clear.

I reached my bag and removed my swimsuit. "You take a long enough shower?" My neck nearly snapped. Niles was standing on the other side of the room looking at me. "I guess I'm slow." I quickly wrapped a towel around my exposed body. I didn't fully understand my discomfort. I hadn't been disgusted by Niles' deck changing. *Quite the opposite, actually.* "Well you weren't slow in the water." He put his hand on my shoulder. "Can you do me a favor?" I made the mistake of looking up into his blue eyes.

Foreigners didn't have cars. My freshman year, I could've been nicknamed 'The Chauffeur.' Niles was the first of many to ride shotgun to the bank, movies, or nearest restaurant. Mallory wanted to have a study date after practice. I sent her a quick text saying I would be late. The phone vibrated almost immediately. I didn't check her response.

The drive to and from the bank lasted around thirty minutes. I expected Niles to talk about his past accomplishments or compare the inferior American system of government to that of socialist Sweden. "So, tell me about yourself, Conner," he said.

I told him I was a distance swimmer. That I wanted to train hard and hopefully be valuable to the team.

"I already know that you are a fast swimmer, man. I saw you kicking all of our asses at practice," Niles said. "I want to know about what else you do."

I didn't think there was much about my life that would excite someone like Niles. He was so different compared to me, the small, lanky boy who had just left home for the first time and was scared to death by it. Still, I told him about my mom, dad, and dog. I admitted the college was only twenty minutes from where they lived. If he wasn't interested in what I had to say, he was doing a great job faking. He maintained perfect eye contact and continued to ask questions.

"What do you want to do after school?"

"I've always wanted to publish a book," I said.

"There's no money in writing. I'm going into Economics."

"Yeah writing is more like a hobby anyway. It's cool that you've already chosen a major. I haven't yet. I'll probably do that my sophomore year, probably." I was rambling, but couldn't stop.

He nodded politely and continued the interview. "Are you dating anyone?"

My high school life consisted of me going to morning swim practice, going to school, going to afternoon practice, going home, doing homework, and then going to bed. "I never even had time to kiss a girl."

Mom told me not to tell anyone that I hadn't had my first kiss. She said people would make fun of me. Niles simply flashed a bright white smile. "Don't worry about it, man," he said. "Everyone moves at their own pace."

Niles and I grabbed dinner at a local restaurant. He paid for my meal; he said he owed me gas. When we returned to campus, the sun had already set. In the dark, I almost didn't see Mallory standing outside my dorm hall. "Where have you been," she said. "I texted you."

Before I could answer with my extended "umm," Niles spoke up. "We had a bro date. We're thinking about a movie now." *We were?*

Mallory put her hand on her hip and attempted a smile. "Conner and I need to study."

I figured Ginger would still be clawing at a piece of yarn tomorrow. "Well, we don't have any homework. A movie sounds nice." Mallory scrunched her face. "Do you want to join us?"

"Depends on what movie. I might have seen it."

"You probably have," Niles said. "Come on, Conner."

I followed him away from Mallory. I thought about telling her I'd come over after the movie, but I couldn't do it with Niles hovering over me. "That girl needs to chill the fuck down," he said, once we were far enough away.

***

His room had a distinct scent to it. It didn't smell good or bad. It was just different. The room itself was considerably messy. It contained items of clothing and old pieces of paper scattered across the floor. It didn't seem possible. School was only three weeks in and I didn't hear any reports of earthquakes in the area.

We ended up watching two movies. A Swedish feature, *The Girl with the Dragon Tattoo,* and an American classic, *Good Will Hunting.* I didn't have homework, but we did have morning practice. I wanted to sleep, but I worried if I left, the moment would be lost.

For both movies, Niles had emotion and commentary. When a joke was made he laughed in such an animated way that his entire face turned red. He grabbed his chest, struggling to breathe. When he wasn't laughing, he was reminiscing. *The Girl with the Dragon Tattoo* reminded Niles of many firsts. The first time he masturbated at age twelve or the first time he learned to make his penis move like a helicopter at age fourteen. *Good Will Hunting* reminded him of the movies that he would watch in Sweden. He said that they would be in English, but have Swedish subtitles. According to Niles, that's how he learned to speak English.

Good Will Hunting was a little over halfway finished when Niles fell asleep. He was a quiet sleeper. *It was probably the only time he didn't talk.* He began twitching. He was only in boxers and had kicked the cover off his legs.

My hand brushed against his leg as I pulled the fabric over his body. My fingers trembled as they combed through his leg hair. I tucked the cover below his neckline. *Was his face always this small?* His open mouth emitted soft rhythmic breaths. I lowered myself, and placed a delicate kiss on his check.

***

The next day, I found myself in desperate need to talk to someone. I saw Mallory in Chemistry class. I asked her if we could talk. "That's ok, Conner. You don't need to apologize. I forgive you. It's the Christian thing to do." *Was she upset about the movie incident?* I tried to talk to her again, but she didn't speak to me for the rest of class.

The dungeon's one benefit was that it allowed me to focus solely on swimming. *Right arm, left arm, breath, right arm, left arm, flip turn, streamline, right arm, left arm, breath* . . . I continued the intense training. I found if I continued to finish practice first, I could enter and exit the locker room before Niles and the nudists arrived.

My plan worked for about three weeks. Niles must have worked on his endurance. He finished close behind me and caught me in the locker room. "I was beginning to think you showered somewhere else," he said as he lowered his suit. He asked me if I could drive him to his roommate's soccer game. I had nowhere to avert my gaze. With his blue eyes above and his penis below, he had me trapped . . .

I did my best not to talk during the drive. I hadn't really talked to him since our movie night. His eyes, lips, thin cheek bones; just looking at him made me feel dirty.

When we arrived, Niles stayed in the car. "You want to tell me what's bothering you?"

For a long time, the thought had nestled deep inside

the crevasse of my mind. Shrouded in shadows, but growing like a tumor. Since the kiss, the thought had taken shape. It took the form of words, continuously repeating inside my mind. But never aloud. "I think I'm . . ." I paused. Like water had filled my lungs, I couldn't breathe. "Gay."

In my head I anticipated several diverse reactions I might receive, but I never expected his. "I know," he said. "I made a bet with myself on how long it would take for you to tell me."

"And you don't care?"

"Of course not," he said. "And if anyone ever gives you any kind of shit about it, they can go fuck themselves!"

We never made it to the soccer game. That night, I told him things I had never shared with anyone. There were several things I feared; my parents, friends, religion. I questioned the life I would live. All the while, he listened patiently.

He only asked one question. "Do you like anyone?"

Of course! "No."

He leaned closer. "Really?"

I answered as honestly as I felt capable. "I had a small crush on you when we first met."

"And why wouldn't you," he said. "I'm pretty hot!"

***

What started as the most intimate conversation I had ever experienced, soon fizzled back into petty awkwardness. For weeks, I tensed each time Niles was around. I didn't know what to say to him. I didn't know whether to act like our conversation never happened or whether I could talk with him about my sexuality more.

I started showering with the team. I kept my eyes locked on myself (and occasionally Niles). Inclusion in team showers soon segued to inclusion in team meals. After practice dinners in the school cafeteria became a routine. One night, Niles was entertaining us with a story about his trip to Paris. About halfway through our meal, I heard a familiar voice calling out to me. "Hey Conner," Mallory said. She squeezed into the seat between me and Niles.

"After that," Niles said. "This French guy comes up to me and tells me how sexy I am. He tried to show me what he called 'work pics.' I was afraid to say, 'fuck you' because I thought he might get the wrong idea."

Everyone but Mallory burst into laughter.

"I would think you would take someone liking you as a complement." I said.

"It's just a joke, Conner. Stop being so awkward."

Awkward?

Mallory flared. "The only awkward thing was that story."

Niles ignored her. "I'm done," he said. "Let's go boys." He and the other swimmers left. I stayed with Mallory.

"You don't have to let Niles push you around. He's a jerk," Mallory said.

"He's not really."

"I think he is, and I think you're better than him. You're smart and you're nice, Conner. People tell me all the time how sweet they think you are." She placed her hand lightly on mine. *Maybe I could talk to Mallory?* Then she continued. "He's a bad influence. I have a religion class with him. God punishes atheists, Conner." She thumbed her cross necklace.

I spent the rest of the night with Mallory. We watched more tributes to Ginger, including episodes of her climbing a fence and making an impressive five-foot leap. In between Ginger trying to catch a red dot and running into a screen door, Mallory inserted a thirty-minute talk show about Jesus. All the while, she twirled the cross between her fingers. The entire time, I imagined Ginger choking on it.

***

With swim season picking up, I found myself doing everything I could to be around Niles. Adrenaline splashed through my veins when we interacted.

"Can we expect you home this weekend?" Mom asked during her traditional weekly call. "We're grilling steaks with the neighbors."

"Sorry, Niles and I are having another movie marathon."

"Just the two of you?"

"We may ask a couple of other friends." *He invited the whole swim team, actually.*

"Just be careful." I heard my heartbeat during the brief silence. "This guy may be looking for a green card." She laughed. "He does know you don't have a sister?"

I ended the call and opened my photos. The most recent picture featured my, fully uniformed, swim team gathered around the dungeon's diving blocks. I zoomed in on Niles who stood atop one of the blocks, sporting a blue and yellow speedo. My hand slipped into my pants as I imagined him slowly caressing the swimsuit down his body. For a moment, I pictured the two of us standing parallel, wearing a different kind of suit.

My parents still didn't know I was gay. To them, Niles was a frustrating, but harmless man-crush. Mallory saw him differently. The day after my Conference swim meet, she pulled me aside.

"We haven't had a study session in weeks."

"Swimming takes a lot of my time."

"What about tonight? Didn't the season just end?"

"Niles and I are going to go to a party." I told her tonight was a swim team party to celebrate the end of our season.

Fists on hips, she blocked my exit. "You never liked going to parties before."

"Before what? You didn't even meet me until our first day of college."

"I don't like you drinking. I worry about you." *What was she worried about? People in Sweden could drink at sixteen.* It was probably the light, but at that moment I swore her cross had grown to twice its size. It dangled between her breasts, its increasing weight lowing her to hands and knees.

"I suppose you'd rather me watch your cat shit all over herself?"

"You didn't use to curse." Suddenly, her cross was

normal again. Instead of anger twitching in her eyes, I saw tears.

***

The party was wilder than any other team get together. The drinks were hard liquor and I was positive I smelled weed. I reasoned that the end of the season meant we no longer had to regulate what we put in our bodies.

I found Niles and he invited me to be his beer pong partner. We played against two Americans first. They didn't last. I was impressed with my aim and precision until things started getting a little blurred. My ball started missing the cups, and soon the table altogether.

"That's your first drink," Niles said. "Are you that much of a light weight?"

"Your mom doesn't think so." I laughed.

A team consisting of two Swedish guys approached us. Niles sighed. "I'm going to need a partner who can speak coherently." *I didn't realize I was slurring my words.* "I'll find you later Conner."

I found a nearby chair and watched the game. Niles grabbed another Swede and they commenced. When they won, Niles jumped in place and high-fived his partner. Then the four of them found a couch on the opposite side of the room and began speaking in what I assumed was Swedish.

I waited a few minutes, then crossed the room and sat next to Niles. I stretched my arm along the couch top. It remained there roughly five seconds before sliding onto Niles's back. I felt his shoulders tense for a second, then return to their typical relaxed position. "What are you guys talking about?"

Niles said he and the other Swedish guys were planning a vacation to Florida for Spring Break. He asked if I wanted to join. "Hell yes," I said. I paused to drink more vodka.

***

I didn't talk to Niles much after the end-of-season party. At first, I didn't think anything about it, but then I overheard some girls in Chemistry class talking about the "like totally epic" movie night they had in Niles's room. *He hadn't invited me.* Suddenly, I realized the space between us. He hadn't been texting me. He hadn't been to my room. We didn't have any of the same classes, and we weren't practicing anymore.

I tried texting him to meet up for dinner. Every time, he had already eaten. We were no longer on the same routine.

I thought about asking his advice. *Maybe we could plot strategies on how to obtain my first kiss? Or talk about Spring Break? Or maybe ask him for help saving the school from the giant snake I suspected lived under the campus?* All were nice ideas, but each time I thought to implement one, I concluded it would only annoy him.

I saw him a few times in the cafeteria. He was always surrounded by a bunch of people. When I sat down, I became just one of several individuals on seat's edge waiting for the next thing he had to say. He could tell a story with such energy and excitement that everyone around him would be transfixed. It could be about swimming, school, poop, cup holders . . . Whatever the case, all eyes were on Niles and his eyes worked the room.

One day I found him sitting with just two of my Swedish teammates. *Now's my chance.* I slipped into the vacant seat next to him. "Sup Conner," Niles said. He continued to his conversation, in Swedish. They were all speaking and laughing in a language I couldn't comprehend.

No one translated for me. I ate without speaking.

***

During college, certain things have a way of sneaking up on you. For some it's an Algebra exam, for others it's public safety after one too many drinks, for my freshman year it was Spring Break. It was only two weeks away. I hadn't talked to Niles about it since the party. I really wanted to go to Florida. I stared out my dorm window and envisioned the salty beach water running over my face. *I'd talk to him today.* I checked his usual habitats. This included pretty much anywhere except the library.

Finally, I saw a Swedish swimmer walking across campus. I flagged him down and asked if he'd seen Niles. "Not since yesterday when we planned our trip to the Bahamas."

My chest ached. I felt this strange sensation; like I was . . . hollow. I quickly began to text Niles, 'I need to talk with you, it's important.' He responded almost instantly and told me to meet him in the cafeteria. He was alone when I found him.

I didn't know exactly how or where to begin. "I heard that you decided to go to the Bahamas."

Niles continued to eat. He didn't speak.

"I thought that you wanted to go to Florida."

He looked at me for a second. *Could he see my hands trembling?* At that moment, I realized I was scared of him. *No, not scared.* I was terrified of what he was going to say.

"We decided on the Bahamas. You didn't help us plan. I assumed you didn't want to go anymore."

"I didn't really get a chance to talk to you. I tried to, but you were always busy."

"There are other guys going. They could've helped you just as well as me. You could have told me you wanted to talk about the vacation, but you didn't."

I tried to find the right words to say, but I couldn't think of anything.

"And honestly, Conner, I'm not saying this to be a dick, but I told you about the trip when I was drunk. You're a liability."

"A liability?"

"I'm two years older than you, and I'm from Sweden. The things that you're dealing with now, I've already dealt with. I'm not gay," he emphasized that sentence. "But as for everything else: I had my first kiss when I was ten, I drank for the first time when I was fourteen, I had sex when I was sixteen. You make such a big deal out of some things when they're no big deal at all."

The hollow feeling in my chest spread throughout my entire body. Sweat dripped from under my armpits. "So, I don't get a spring break on the beach?" I don't know if I was trying to sound sarcastic or angry. It probably came out as neither.

"You don't need my permission. You said your family has a beach house on the west coast. You could go there."

I stared down at the table. "I've considered you my best friend."

"I'm not saying that I'm not your friend. We're just different. You hang out with people, fine people, but people I don't care to be around, like Mallory. No offense, one-on-one, you're fine. In a group, you can get really awkward."

I sat there thinking he was an ass. I thought about how he tricked me. *He only acted like my friend, so he could use my car.* I thought about all the times I drove him to the bank, shopping malls, strip clubs . . . *Places I didn't want to go.* All the plans I canceled in the hopes that he would message me. I thought about how I hated him. But, that wasn't true. The truth was, everything he said made sense.

"Conner," Niles said. "Try to think of me like your

teammate. We swam together, and now swim season is over."

***

The sound of my hand beating against the door echoed through the empty hall. I heard a faint noise inside the room, and finally Mallory opened the door. "What's wrong?" she said. I imagined my face was pretty red.

I sat on her bed. "Niles and I had a fight."

"I know he's important to you." Her voice was calm and nurturing.

I shook my head.

"You guys are just a little stressed. You'll be in Florida soon. You'll relax, and you'll make up."

"I'm not going on the trip. Niles said he didn't want me to go."

She moved her hand to my face. She gently guided me to face her. "I never liked Niles anyway." She pressed our faces together. Our lips met, and I felt the cool wetness of her tongue exploring the inside of my mouth.

I moved my hands up her body and to her breasts. *People had always said she had 'nice tits.'* I squeezed her boobs. They felt interesting, but that was it.

I pulled away from her. "I'm gay, Mallory."

She shook her head. "No, you're not."

"Yes I am."

I still remember the look on her face. It was like nothing I ever saw before or wanted to see again. I wondered if that was how I looked when I had talked with Niles.

***

The pool was closed, but that didn't matter. The side door lock was broken. I pushed the withered door aside and approached the dark body of water. I stripped off my clothes and imagined the sands of Florida beneath my feet.

With open eyes, I took the plunge. The water wrapped around me, streaming over every ounce of flesh on my body. I listened to the waves wrestle each other. I grabbed my legs and sank, flipping as many times as I could before reaching the sandy bottom. Up above, the blurred sun was retiring beneath the dunes.

I curled my toes and pushed, exploding through the surface. The shore was in sight. My arms sliced through the untamed current. A thin sheet of bubbles blew past my face with every stroke. I kicked my legs. There were no coaches, crosses, or teammates. For once, it was only me.

My mind began to race with thoughts of Niles and Mallory. *How had I been so stupid? How could I have done that? What was I thinking? What was going to happen? . . . Why did I care so much?*

I reached the concrete pavement gasping for air but smiling at the same time. My cap and goggles left my face and soared through the windowless enclosure. I rested under the dim prison lights and let the laughter spill out of my lungs. I closed my eyes as the warm salty liquid ran down my face.

My tears dripped into the pool as my laughter echoed through the empty dungeon.

***

I didn't speak to Niles until after he returned from Spring Break. Occasionally, we saw each other in passing and even said, "Hello." Once swim season started the next year, we saw each other more often. We ate dinner together a few times and went to the movies once or twice, but it was never like it was, or at least how I thought it was.

Niles didn't need my attention, but Mallory was

different. *I never wanted to hurt her.* Like Niles, I saw her from time to time. Whenever we bumped into one another we would always smile and talk about how we needed to catch up. I wanted to think we were still friends, but something told me we weren't.

I went to her room one night and told her I didn't mean to lead her on. "Thank you," she said with no more or less meaning behind her words. That night, I watched my last Ginger video. She chased a red dot over the edge of an outdoor pool. In what looked like a new swim technique involving all the strokes, she managed to claw her way to the shallow end.

"I wish I was that fast," I said. Mallory and I shared a laugh.

***

By the end of my senior year, I had officially come out. First, to my parents. That event required weeks of liquid courage. My expectations yielded a night riddled with shouts and broken furniture. The reality proved to be nothing more than a civilized conversation. Though it ended with a friendly reminder from Mom, "Don't feel like you need to share your business with everyone."

A week later, I told the swim team. Once the girls on my team had confirmation, it didn't take long for the entire campus to know. Occasionally, I got a dirty look from some southern boys or had a couple girls from religion class try to read me Bible verses, but all in all, everything was fine.

Weirdly enough, being out of the closet made dating a bit smoother. This lead to a tall blond named Zach. He and I started dating my junior year and had both been accepted into the same graduate school.

My senior year of swimming ended well. Zach cheered me on to break three school records. He even convinced me to wear a Speedo.

"See you in two weeks, Honey," he said. We took off our graduation caps to kiss. I waved bye to him and smiled at the thought of our upcoming trip to my beach house. So many times, I think of how much easier it would have been if that were the end of my college experience . . .

I was in my room packing my bags when I heard a knock. I opened the door to a six foot, two inch Swedish boy with muddy blond hair and piercing blue eyes. He needed to catch the five o'clock flight back to Sweden. It was already

2:00. *Typical.* I was surprised he asked me because he knew several other people with cars, but I agreed to, once again, don 'The Chauffeur' persona.

On the way, he asked what my plans were now that I finished college and I asked him what he was going to do back in Sweden. We talked a lot about traveling. He said that he might come back to the United States, but probably not. He wanted to go to Australia.

Just before we arrived, he asked about Zach. He and I had not talked about anything regarding my sexuality since our freshman year. I told him that we were doing well and of our plans to go to grad school together.

"That's good. I'm glad that you found someone right for you. You're a good person, Conner."

That car ride was destined to be the last time I ever saw or spoke to Niles. At times, I remember it with regret. Regret that I spent my freshman year obsessed with a man that would never love me back, regret that I badmouthed him my sophomore year, regret that at times when I was with Zach I envisioned Niles in his place . . .

No matter how much time passed, I could close my eyes and once again sit in the car with him and confess my secret. A secret that at the time defined me. No matter what my future held, he would always be the first person I ever shared that part of my life with.

He stood there, luggage by his side. I extended my hand to him. I don't remember if the wind was blowing or if the sun was out. But I remember him pulling me into a hug. I buried my head into his shoulder. I didn't look, but I knew he was crying. I relived that moment over and over. *Maybe there was something I could say to make him stay? Maybe I could have kept our friendship?* Instead, I squeezed him tighter and listened as he said, "Come visit me if you're ever in Sweden."

The
Beach at Sunset

He asked me to be his boyfriend on a beach at sunset. Riley told me he wanted to go to the coast. "Your wish is my command," I had said. My grandmother lived out her retirement in a small house on a humble island by the west coast. I spent my summers growing up on the island, and had inherited the house when she passed.

Riley had held me close. An earlier rain shower had sent everyone away. We were the only two left as far as the eye could see. I had turned to look at the ocean right as the tip of the sun hit the edge of the water. Light glistened over the sea, waving with the tides. The light stretched over the sand dunes and centered on us.

It was a beautiful moment. It reminded me of the night my best friend, Zeke, and I went skinny dipping. It was the first time I saw a penis which wasn't mine. It was shriveled from the cool water, but that was somehow charming. Perhaps it was then when I first knew I was gay. Before the open water, he and I stretched out on the sand and waited hours for the sun to disappear beneath the ocean line. From the moment it touched the sea, its glow spread over the shifting waters and seemed to engulf the entire island. Zeke and I didn't often speak to each other during sunsets. We didn't need words.

Zeke lived on the island, but wasn't around when Riley and I got together. Since I went to college, I'd seen less of Zeke. I never even told him I was gay. I'd wanted to introduce Zeke to Riley. I guess that wasn't going to happen now. I thought about what he would say. *Would he be surprised?* He'd probably just smile and say "Cool, want to go for a swim?"

I stood on the sand with my phone, checking its camera in vain. We'd been too slow driving, I'd just missed the sunset. In the on-setting darkness, the water was barely distinguishable from the sand through my phone's camera. I closed the camera and opened the texts from my last conversation with Riley:

'Are you sure you don't want to come with us? They'd be happy to have you.'

'We should probably talk . . . Tell Kane I'm sorry.'

I sighed and started walking back to the house. *It would be fine.* I'd go back, and we'd have shrimp; shrimp from the sea. The sunset could wait one more day.

It was the first night of a celebratory beach trip. I'd just finished my first season with my university's swim club. Riley told me I was crazy trying to swim while getting a PhD. I had placed my hand on his cheek. "I swam varsity in undergrad. Club swimming isn't nearly as intense. You'll see, I'll still have time for you."

Riley never understood what swimming meant to me. It was more than a sport, it was my lifestyle. The water was always there for me when I needed it. I swam 10 miles the day my grandmother was diagnosed with cancer. I spent the day practicing dives when I was rejected from my top choice of graduate school. When things ended with my first boyfriend, I sat in the ocean and let it rock me. Being on a team also gave me the opportunity to make friends who shared that common interest.

I'd invited some guys from my team to my beach

house. We'd have the weekend to relax and I'd have the chance to think. When we arrived Ashton and Quinn had sprinted to grab the two guest bedrooms. Kane quietly took the couch. Since he didn't have a bathroom, I said he could share with me.

Quinn was the largest of my friends and by far the least talkative. Quinn reserved his efforts for the things in life most important to him; namely swimming, history, and locating the ideal place to smoke a joint.

Ashton was the only foreigner in our group. My first-ever boyfriend insisted that I was obsessed with foreign swimmers. His thoughts had some merit. Foreign swimmers did fascinate me. We came from different worlds yet shared our common sport. We knew the struggles of morning practice, weekend competitions, and the smell of chlorine that never seemed to completely evaporate from our skin. It was like we spoke our own common language.

Kane was top of his class, fit-bodied, and the second-best swimmer on our team. Furthermore, he exhibited the well-balanced mixture of confidence, awkwardness, and just enough niceness to have several prospective girlfriends. When Riley and I started dating, he made it clear that his weekends weren't reserved for my swimming competitions.

After getting a glimpse of Kane in a speedo, his attendance substantially improved. "You must be the only person in the world who doesn't think he's hot," Riley said. I told him that I found Kane's body, much like his personality, a little too basic. I told myself inviting Kane was a good thing. We shared the same team, the same lane during practice, and the same group of friends. Therefore, we should be friends.

***

The next morning, I woke up to the smell of crisp banana pancakes. Ashton prepared multiple stacks for all of us. "It was the least I could do," he smiled. "Thanks for letting us stay here."

Ashton, Quinn, and I sat down to breakfast. I noticed Kane's absence. The ruffled couch cushions and blankets scattered on the floor indicated he had left and was putting off tidying up.

About twenty minutes later, Kane barged through the front door. He was shirtless and dripping what I hoped was ocean water. The liquid seemed concentrated on his uppermost body. The droplets clung to his face, neck, and the patch of hair between his nipples, but was almost repelled by the smoothness of his stomach. I averted my gaze to the ground. From the knee down, his legs were coated in sand, which he proceeded to track across the floor. "Where have you been," I asked.

"I went for a swim. I got to see the sunrise from the ocean. Man, it was beautiful."

"I know," I said. "I did grow up here." I must have sounded harsher than I'd intended. Quinn and Ashton briefly paused their breakfast and Kane raised his eyebrow. I continued in a lighter tone. "What's really beautiful is the sunset. It goes directly into the ocean. Growing up, my friend Zeke and I watched the sunset all the . . ."

"You mind if I use the shower?" Kane called from the bathroom. He left before hearing the end of my story, which was fine; he didn't need to experience the sunset.

"Make sure you get all the sand out when you finish," I shouted back. The water was already running. I accepted that, just like the now sandy floor, it was my mess to clean.

I asked the guys if they wanted to come to the beach with me. Ashton and Quinn accepted. Kane said he would join us after he had breakfast. We walked down the gravel road leading from my house to the shore. "That's Zeke's house," I said, gesturing to the small stilted home at the end of the street. The structure had hosted several late-night conversations, and apparently since I'd gone to college, seance circles. "He's not here this week." There were no cars in the driveway. "I guess his mom is on vacation." Quinn and Ashton eyed the house for a moment, before erasing it from their memories and continuing forward.

Walking across the boardwalk over the sand dunes, I began to smell the salty air. I heard the water crashing upon itself. The water itself was majestic. It was like a person: beautiful on the outside with secrets in its depths that no one, not even those closest to it, would ever fully know.

When we found a place on the sand, Quinn asked me if beach patrol covered the entire island. I said they usually didn't check past a mile south. He said he would be back.

Ashton and I sat in the warm sun. We watched the waves break in silence. I attempted to write some story ideas in my journal while simultaneously digging a hole with my feet.

"So, I was thinking of asking Monica to move in with me." Ashton said after a while. "We've been dating two and a half years. That's not too early, right?"

I shook my head. "Riley and I have been dating for less

than that and we may move in together after graduation."

"Really? How are things between you guys?"

"Fine. He's just been really busy."

"That's why you said he couldn't come with us, right?"

"Well you know how he stresses about work." I dug my feet deeper into the hole and paused to cover them with more sand. "He's always concerned about his busy schedule."

"I haven't heard him say too much about it. But I really only get to see him at swim meets and he mostly just talks to you and Kane."

"I feel like he tries to talk to everyone."

"He gives Kane more attention though. It makes sense. I always find myself talking to Monica's most attractive friends."

I pulled my feet out of the sand and started digging a new hole. I pushed harder this time. "I don't get why everyone thinks Kane is so hot. I guess he's "technically" attractive." I gestured air quotes. "But it's almost like he's too attractive; like so much that he's not. You know how some people are so fun that hanging out with them becomes less fun?"

"No. You can be so fun that it's overwhelming and exhausting, but you're still fun." He paused and took a long sip of his water. I stopped digging my feet and leaned closer to Ashton. His face was serious, like he needed my attention for something important. "People like to be around attractive people. That's why you like to be around me."

"Please." I scooped a piece of sand and threw it on his chest. "I'm so out of your league it's not even funny." He waited until I put my journal down to throw his water on me.

Kane eventually joined us. He didn't bring a chair, beach towel, or even a shirt. I asked if anyone wanted to go swimming. Ashton said he didn't want to swim, but he would water wrestle. Kane said he wanted to tan and asked if he could use my chair.

Ashton and I took off our shirts and ran into the water. It was cold. I hesitated before diving under. The current was strong; it pulled me down. I swam against it. I won.

I emerged from the water. Ashton grabbed me from behind and tackled me under. I was submerged in the salt water. I could feel the waves, like a gust of wind, breaking above the surface and gliding over me. I was held by Ashton, but I felt free. I felt like a child, floating through the sea one last time with my best friend.

I used my feet and pushed Ashton into the current. He collided with a breaking wave and was forced under. When he emerged, I tackled him again. While pinning Ashton under the water, I glanced over at Kane. Still sunbathing. Clearly his appearance was top priority. Riley would have certainly agreed. For a moment, I questioned why I invited Kane.

Ashton broke free. He seized my shoulders and hurled me into an oncoming wave. Big mistake. I caught the wave mid-break and rode into Ashton, taking out his legs. He fell on top of me. The ocean had us now. Together we rolled through the shallow water, bending to the will of the wave. I emerged unscathed. Ashton stood up gradually; his face half coated in sea mud and swim trunks struggling to maintain their grasp.

"Having some trouble?" I laughed. He flipped me off.

I looked again towards Kane. He was watching us. His lips were curled into a light smile. The kind that occurs by instinct, just barely showing teeth. He appeared to be laughing with me.

***

A few hours before the sun was scheduled to set, my team convinced me to 'elevate' myself with them. "Trust me, it'll make the sun's glow that much brighter." Quinn said. We sat in a circle on my back porch. Quinn supplied the joints,

Ashton the beer, Kane the wine, and I the porch. I was impressed with my team's tolerance. Together we hit eight joints, a dozen beers, and a large bottle of wine. I don't know who had what, but I only took half a joint and one beer. I didn't make a habit of smoking, or drinking for that matter. I'd been so focused on my swim season that I'd repressed many things.

We smoked and drank for a couple hours, exchanging stories about life and plans for after school. "I'm going to get a big house in Washington," Quinn said. He leaned back in his chair and exhaled a black cloud. "It'll have a bunker too. I'll be ready for World War 4."

"Not worried about 3?" I asked.

"We're already living in 3. They just don't want to tell us yet. The word 'war' scares people, causes a panic, you know?"

Ashton talked about moving east. He was getting some kind of engineering degree, electric or mechanical. I couldn't remember, but either way he'd be secure in the job market. Kane briefly mentioned moving into a city to use his economics degree. I didn't realize we were studying the same field. Kane nodded along as I talked about my classes and how I met Riley on my first internship.

As the empty beer bottles accumulated, the conversation became slightly more personal. "I beat it in my grandma's basement. Her cats were staring at me, it was fucking weird," Quinn said.

"My most awkward place was the YMCA parking lot," Ashton said. "I was under a blanket in my car. Several people walked by. I tried to pretend to look at my phone so no one would notice."

"Mine was on a beach," Kane said. "I went deep into the water and yanked it." I perked up. I never thought of Kane as the type to find the beach stimulating. An image came to mind of him standing in the water, jerking his hand with the tides, and letting the cum flow into the waves.

"Mine was also the beach," I said. "However, I wasn't in the water."

"You found a place all alone out in the open?" Kane seemed impressed. Though I wasn't alone. I closed my eyes and flashed back to a time just after sunset. My hand in my swim trunks and eyes looking directly into his. Zeke was focused on me as well, his face scrunched until he finally came. In that moment when his face loosened and a smile crept across his lips, I wondered what he was thinking. I'd give anything to know.

When the time for the sunset approached, I left the elevation circle to head for the beach. I asked if anyone wanted to join me. "I'm good man," Ashton said. Quinn nodded in agreeance and then went back to talking about the French Revolution.

"I'll go with you," Kane said. "Just let me change clothes." I followed him inside and watched him take off his sweaty shirt and throw it on my couch. He piled a few more articles of clothing on there, before finding the t-shirt he wanted. "I still can't get over what a great first season you had, man." Kane said. "Especially your 1000 Meter."

"Thanks. I was surprised I broke the team record."

"It was actually my record." Kane's head was successfully through the t-shirt's head hole. It hung around his neck, he wasn't attempting to secure his arms. *Was he expecting an apology?* "I was wondering if you wanted to train together sometime? It'd be a good way to stay in shape since the season's over, and you might teach me a thing or two."

It honestly sounded great, but I knew I couldn't swim with him one on one. "I'm not sure I'll have time. I'm signing up for some cooking classes now that the season's over. Riley thinks I need serious help. He hates my signature dish, canned soup."

"You did remember to take the soup out of the can, right?"

"Shit. Are you always supposed to do that?" We both laughed. I didn't remember Kane ever joking around during swim practice. He always seemed so focused. His shirt was now all the way on. He then took off his pants. At this point I was used to guys changing in front of me. I'd seen Kane, Ashton, and Quinn's manhood and more.

"I could teach you how to cook. We could train after classes and then make dinner at my house?"

"I'll think about it," I smiled to myself. I'd sworn after my college experience swimming, that I would never date a swimmer. It was just too complicated. My commitment to do so, however, did deprive me of certain things. I'd always fantasized about finishing a practice with my boyfriend and then going out to dinner afterward. We'd talk about our training and eat like pigs without judgement.

"How are things with Riley?"

Why did people keep asking that? "He's fine, busy."

"You guys are lucky. I'd be in a relationship too if girls didn't find me so damn awkward."

"Trust me. Several people find you attractive." He took a moment to stretch his legs into a white swimsuit. I had

54

to admit he had nice thighs; toned and tanned enough to make his blond hair almost invisible.

"Looks aren't my problem," He said a little too quickly. "Girls approach me all the time, but after five minutes of talking, they get scared off."

"Well, it's been five minutes and I'm still here." I tapped my Apple Watch. Suddenly, I remembered. "Shit, the sunset." I ran to the window. It was still light outside, but the sun was almost completely swallowed by the sea. We were a five-minute walk from the beach. Even if I ran I wouldn't get a good picture. "Damn it! I needed to take a picture for him."

"We can just get a pic tomorrow?"

"We'll leave tomorrow before the sunset. This is just great. Zeke was counting on me!"

"Who's Zeke?"

I realized what I'd done. "I meant Riley. Zeke is my friend, he lives on the island."

"Cool. Do we get to meet him?"

"He's not here right now. If you listened to me, you would have known that."

"Sorry." He tapped his fingers against his thigh and exhaled. "It's still light out; do you want to head to the beach?"

"You go ahead. I'll stay here and clean my shower. You tracked in a lot of sand."

"Oh, I can clean it out."

"For the love of God Kane, go to the damn beach!"

Kane snatched his beer and let the door slam as he left for the porch. I decided to clean the shower. I might as well let my adrenaline be productive. It was messier than I thought. The shell white tub was plastered with dark patches of sand. Running the water didn't seem to help. The sand just soaked it up. I eventually got the bathroom sponge and cleaning soap. I lathered the tub and scrubbed the stagnant sand. *There was no way Kane would do a good job cleaning this. He'd just say he would do it tomorrow. It must be nice to always have tomorrow.*

When I finished, I made my way to the porch. Ashton sat alone in a rocking chair. A beer in one hand and a phone in the other. He eyed the phone suspiciously as if trying to alter the contents with his mind. He rolled his eyes before pressing a single button and placing the cellular device in his lap.

"Hey," he said. "I was just sending Monica a picture. I titled it 'Beach Life.' I wasn't sure if she would like that I was drinking."

"Where is everyone?"

"Kane went for a walk." Ashton took a sip of his beer. "Quinn went with him. They're probably going to take some more hits. It'll probably help Kane calm down."

I sighed. "Were we being loud?"

"You weren't being quiet."

"I was probably being an ass." I crossed my arms for a second and bit my lip. Suddenly, I got angry again. "I just wanted to see the sunset. Did he have to take his sweet time changing?"

Under the dim porch light, I could just make out Ashton's face. It was sympathetic, but not indulging. "You know, Kane was nervous when you invited him."

"What'd he have to be nervous about?"

"Well, have you given him a reason to think you don't want him here?" Ashton smirked in such a way that I felt the need to both lightly smile and avoid eye contact. "You ever think there's a reason you're pushing Kane away?"

"What do you mean?"

He smiled. "Never mind." He patted the chair next to him. I sat and took another beer. "You know I asked Monica to marry me a few months ago. She said she wasn't ready."

Before he spoke I considered telling him, but he had

his own drama. My head was swirling with thoughts. In a way, it seemed easier to keep them inside rather than acknowledge their existence. "I had no idea. Sorry, I've been pretty wrapped up in my life."

"We all are." He took another sip, then laughed. I gazed into the darkened sky. There wasn't even a trace of sunlight anymore.

***

I sat in bed clutching the phone. I scrolled through my camera roll. It was a new phone. There weren't any pictures of Zeke, just my swim team and Riley. I needed a picture of the sunset, our sunset. I needed to remember the good times.

There was a knock at my door. I quickly turned off my phone and placed it on the nightstand. "Who is it?"

"Kane. I just wanted to brush my teeth."

Fuck, we're sharing a bathroom. I hadn't seen him since his walk. I tried to wait up for him, but it grew late and I no longer had the energy to give an apology. When I opened the door, he was smiling. It wasn't friendly or happy. It seemed almost nervous.

"Enter away, good sir." I gestured a path with my

hands. He stepped inside and I shut the door behind him. "Look Kane, I wanted to say . . ."

"Conner, I'm sorry. I know seeing the sunset was important to you. I'm sorry we missed it."

"Don't worry about it." I cleared my throat and glanced at the window. "I'm sorry too. I was being . . ."

He cut me off. "It's fine."

I nodded. Neither Kane nor I spoke. It was a strange noise that filled the room. It wasn't silence. Really, everything seemed louder; the clock's steady ticking, the outside wind waving through the tree branches, the soft hum of the air conditioning . . . These sounds penetrated the room and filled the space between us.

"Good," Kane finally said. "I guess I'll go brush my teeth." He walked halfway to the bathroom, stopped, and whipped around. "Are you alright? You seem off." His voice was soft, but stern.

"Everyone would seem off to you. How many joints have you had?"

"Whatever it is you can tell me. We're friends."

"We are, aren't we? I heard you were nervous to come here." My palms were shaking. *Was I nervous too?*

"Of course, we're friends. I wouldn't have come here

if we weren't." He sighed and looked down for a second. "I'll admit when you first joined the team, I wasn't sure if I'd like you. I used to be the fastest swimmer. But you were so nice. I mean you let us stay here despite me trashing the place. Even your boyfriend is friendly. That text was sweet."

Riley had Kane's number? "What text?"

"He sent me a message saying sorry he couldn't come, but he hoped we had a good time. I'm assuming he sent it to everyone?"

Doubt it. "I'm sure he did. He can be very friendly."

He leaned against the door. He had put a decent amount of alcohol and pot in his body. I imagined the lean was done partly for dramatic effect and partly to maintain stability. "I haven't dated much. I hope I find someone like you did. Someone who is nice to my friends and loves me." He pushed himself off the wall and back on his two feet. "I didn't mean to say love. I mean I don't know if you guys have said it yet . . . I'm sorry . . . God." He placed his fingers to his forehead and shut his eyes. "See, this is why I don't get dates." He laughed quietly with his teeth still together.

"Do you remember our first swim team party?" I asked.

"Yeah, the one where you and I had the beer funnel

race! Who ended up winning?"

I did. "No idea. Anyway, it was that night I told Riley I loved him."

"Really, was he there?"

"No, he was here with some friends. I let him use the house. He was pretty mad at me because I said I had too much homework to come, but I still went to the swim party."

"I mean one party doesn't take nearly as much time as a beach trip. Plus, you were doing him a favor."

"Exactly! But he was still mad. I called him after I left the party. It was late, I probably woke him up. I was a little drunk, which only made it worse. I told him he didn't have a right to be angry. 'You're an ass sometimes' I said. 'But I still love you.'"

"Damn! That's one way to do it."

"I shouldn't have said it to him then. I didn't mean it, but he said it back to me. I didn't know what to do after that. He said it all the time; after every phone call, every time he left my apartment, even in front of my parents. Eventually he commented on how I never seemed to say it back."

"What did you do?"

"I just waited until I knew I loved him. It sounds cheesy, but I knew after the first time we had sex." Though I thought the same about my first boyfriend. They were the only two I'd ever been with.

"What's it like?"

"To be in love?" I contemplated how to put the emotion into words. *Was it even an emotion? Did I know it well enough to dissect it?*

"No, I meant sex . . ." He hesitated. "You know, guy on guy . . . Sorry, I was just . . ."

"You're fine." I rubbed my eyes, suddenly feeling the exhaustion behind them. "It's not as painful as you would think. It's not really comfortable, but there's a weird kind of pleasure to the discomfort."

"Interesting." His tongue massaged his teeth. "Well, it's late. I should probably be getting to my couch." Kane spun around and trotted to the bathroom. When he emerged, he examined his teeth in the bedroom mirror. "Good as new!" He clicked his teeth in what I believe was an attempt to exemplify his brushing skills. "Thanks again for letting us stay here."

"Anytime. I honestly am happy you came."

He opened his arms. Surprised, I tilted my head and scrunched my face. To which he responded "Come on! We just had a heart to heart, we've got to hug it out."

I approached his body slowly. As we made contact, our chests pressed against each other. His arms went around my back and pushed me further into him. I could hear him breathing. I could feel his heart beat. A feeling entered my body. Like the air was going past my lungs. It seeped into my stomach and extended down until it reached my penis. I could feel it tingling, rising . . .

I pulled away. My senses heightened, and I was doing my best to ignore them. "Good night," I said.

"You too." With that he left, and shut the door behind himself.

Leaning against the wooden frame, I shoved my hand in my pants and imagined myself making love to Kane. We'd start with a conversation, probably like the one we just had. However, this time I'd be holding him. I'd start with his thigh. Rubbing it slowly at first, I'd make my way under the trim of his boxer-briefs. We'd kiss. Our lips would quiver at first, but soon find stability as our tongues explored each other's mouths. I'd think of Riley. He'd be there too, watching. Things would move faster. I'd grip Kane tighter. We'd kiss harder. We'd fall to the floor. Kissing. Clutching! ThruSTING! ROLLING!! HOLDING!!! RELEASING . . .

I exhaled. I'd been frequently masturbating lately.

Initially, I tried to focus on celebrities, my ex, or Zeke; people out of my life. For a moment, I wondered if Kane was on the other side of the door having similar thoughts. *It's just physical,* I told myself . . . as I always did.

***

I didn't sleep that night. I laid awake staring at the ceiling. No real thoughts came to mind. Just white ceiling tiles.

No one heard me slip out the front door, or if they did, I imagined they soon forgot and fell back into slumber. It was still dark when I left. I didn't need the light though, I knew the way.

I passed Zeke's house. The driveway was still empty. It made sense. I couldn't imagine a mother wanting to stay in a house where her son overdosed. I don't know why I didn't tell my friends about his death. Maybe for the same reason I didn't tell them the truth about Riley.

I thought about what it was like for Zeke. They say his heart stopped in his sleep. *Was it painless? If you die in your sleep does your dream turn into a nightmare? The kind where you are falling but don't wake up before you hit the ground.* Life had been tough for him. *Did he know what he was doing?*

He had been so happy when we were kids. When we were young and I wasn't so busy.

I walked and thought. I thought and walked. I walked until I reached the sandy edge of the water. I stripped off my clothes and plunged into the ocean. It wasn't cold this time.

The current was stronger than before. The water broke around my fist. It felt so smooth gliding over my bare skin. I slammed my fists into the sea. The water parted, erupting before me. Several small waves approached. I punched harder. I punched Riley. I watched him squirm as he disappeared into the foamy tides. I punched Kane in the jaw. That's what he deserved for ruining the sunset. I punched Quinn, Ashton, and Zeke. Riley came again and I slapped him open-handed. The water feared me. It bent to my will.

I punched and punched until I finally lost my footing and slipped into the strong current. It dragged me under water, but couldn't hold me for long. I escaped and broke through the top of water. Gasping for breath, I saw it. A wave, larger than all the other ones combined. They were working together this time. With no time to react, I closed my eyes and let Poseidon take his best shot.

I was thrust once again under the dark abyss. The liquid flowed over my pulsing veins. I wasn't scared. Up there, the world was unpredictable and out of control. But here, beneath the surface, I was a god.

The current thrust me through the water. Like a hand, it clutched my throat and shoved me deeper into its depths. I remained limp. Escape was still possible. I needed to wait longer. I needed to see where the water would take me.

I rose to the surface long enough to draw a quick breath before water seeped into my lungs and forced me under once more. The smell of the ocean filled my nostrils and seeped into my brain. I could feel the water beating against the inside of my rib cage. The air was almost gone. I needed more time. *Just a little longer*, I thought. *Just . . . a little . . . longer . . .*

Suddenly, I knew. Floating in the dark seclusion, clutching to life I finally had the answer. This was what Zeke felt. He battled with death, so he could see if life was worth living. *Did he choose death? Or did he challenge death and lose?*

The current seized me again, this time around my torso. It clutched me tight and dragged me forward. I couldn't escape now. The current was too powerful. It dragged me until I felt the heels of my feet collide with sand. Something felt weird. The sand seemed to shift upward, as if the current were pushing me towards the shallow water. My face burst through the water surface and I gasped for air. It wasn't the current that had me, it was a pair of hands.

Once I reached the beach, the hands released my chest and spun me around. My vision was blurry, but I could just make out Kane's face. It seemed to explode with rage. "You idiot!"

He shoved me. In a daze, I fell to the ground and began hacking up seawater. The dry heaves burned the inside of my throat with every cough.

"You're so fucking stupid!" He continued to yell. I felt his hand connect with my face. The sound echoed through the sand dunes, but I felt nothing. He stood over me panting. I tried to tell him to relax, that I was fine, but no words came. Instead, I continued to cough. Eventually, I heard a thud as Kane collapsed beside me.

"What were you thinking? You could have killed yourself!"

I continued staring at the sand. The millions of grains seemed so distinct now. A single drop of salty water fell from my face and mixed with the sand. The grains hardened around the droplets, solidifying as they consumed the water. Perhaps if I waited long enough, they would consume me too.

"He's dead," I said still not averting my gaze from the sand. "Zeke killed himself a month ago. I didn't tell Riley. He'd feel sorry for me. I didn't want to force him to stay."

I felt Kane's hand make contact with my face. This time, there was no accompanying sound. His touch lingered and slowly guided my face until it was level with his. He no longer looked angry. Gently, he pressed his lips to mine. I kissed him back as we buried ourselves in the moist sand.

The next morning, we listened to the ocean in silence. It was calm now, flowing with the light breeze. Together, we watched the sun rise.

DIRTY LAUNDRY

Your lips were wet from champagne. You licked them twice over before setting your glass down. During those moments, there was nothing else. It was just you, me, and the dim porch light of your bedroom balcony. It hummed in rhythm to our conversation.

We were talking about things beyond our years and drinking things even further beyond. I didn't even shiver in the cool breeze of the night. All I could focus on was you. Everything about you was what I wished I could be. I wanted dark eyes. I needed your smile. You were perfection when you smiled; cheeks raised, dimples exposed.

"Do you think we will make friends," you slurred.

I knew you were talking about high school. It was all

you talked about for weeks. You counted down the days, hours, and minutes. I looked at my watch. *3 days, 8 hours, 12 minutes.* I only knew because it was an hour since your last countdown announcement.

"Why wouldn't we?" I said.

"We were in private school our whole lives. Don't people get beaten up for that?"

"That's just a stereotype," I laughed.

"No, it's true. My dad told me he used to beat up private school kids. You and I will just have to stick together." I thought you were reaching for my hand, but it was only for the champagne glass.

"We always have."

"But no matter who we meet," you said. "We must always be friends."

"We will."

"And we'll still have sleepovers. I don't care who laughs at us. We'll be those geeky private school girls who still have sleepovers. But we'll be together. That's all that matters. Mom won't care if you come over, she loves you."

Maybe I should have questioned how much you had to drink? Your mother had no idea I was here. She was out of town. Maybe I should have questioned when you mentioned your dad. You never mentioned him before.

"Do you think I'm pretty?" You asked.

I had to wonder if you knew what kind of question you were asking. On some level, I thought you did. I answered as honestly as I could. "I wish I was as beautiful as you."

You crossed your legs in such a way that would turn the head of any boy in our class. "I think you're pretty. I've always loved your hair. I wish I was blonde."

I couldn't see you as a blonde. Your black hair was one of your most defining features. It made you look mysterious.

I said your hair was beautiful. I told you not to change it. But it didn't matter. This whole night was destined to be a blur. Everything; the drinks, the porch, the crisp air . . . wouldn't even be a memory to you.

The next morning, you'd shield your eyes from the sun. I'd hold your hair and you would drink from the kitchen faucet. I knew this because, unlike you, this wasn't my first time drinking. You'd ask what we did. I'd say, "We talked." You'd say, "That's nice." And that would be the end.

I'd never be able to describe our night. How could I put into words the way the flickering porch light left your face half shrouded in darkness? I couldn't do justice to your smile. The way it created thick dimples with pockets impenetrable by the light. They looked bottomless, hypnotically so.

"I should be blonde," you said. "My dad always had a thing for blondes. He told me so." You took another gulp from your third or fourth glass. "I know Mom's not blonde, but the color of her hair wasn't why she did it."

I could tell you wanted something. You *needed* me to respond. And of course, I did. "What did your mother do?"

"She killed my father."

You sounded so serious, I couldn't help but laugh.

"It's true!" You leaned back in the chair and ran your fingers through your long hair. You always did that when you were annoyed. For a moment we were silent. The only noise was the hum of the porch light.

"Yeah, she killed him." You spoke like you were assuring yourself more than me. "Not sure how she did it though. Probably poisoned him or something. When I was younger, I used to think she hid the body somewhere in the house."

I planted my glass on the clear table. The sound echoed through the wind. I hoped it would be enough to snap you back to reality, *half hoped*. "Your mother is a big-time lawyer."

"That's how she got away with it. I know she did it.

She told me."

You weren't going to remember this. It couldn't hurt to play along. "Why did she do it?"

"Dirty laundry."

"What?"

"**Dirty laundry**. He left too much dirty laundry lying around. Mom said he never cleaned up."

"Your mother killed her husband because he was messy?"

"I'm not sure they were married. I have her last name." You took another, longer, sip. "Anyway, it was more than him being messy. He never cleaned up his messes. She always had to. I think it got to be too much for her. She said he would leave all his dirty laundry out in plain sight. She worried the neighbors might see."

"So, she just snapped and decided to kill him?"

"Sort of. She came home early from work one day. That's where she caught him."

"What was he doing?"

"He was making a mess. He had a friend over. She was helping him try on shirts in the bedroom. Mom said he just threw all his unwanted shirts on the floor like they were trash. And the thought of him doing it in front of that woman too.

She had never been so embarrassed. That was when she knew she had to kill him."

The wind was blowing harder now, but I could barely tell. I'd never seen this side to you before. The imagination that you had, the passion for your own words. I didn't want it to end. The story, our sleepovers, the champagne, your flickering porch light . . . They all needed to stay the same.

"Do you think they ever loved each other," I asked.

"Who?"

"**Your parents**. Do you think they were ever in love?"

"How should I know? She killed him while she was pregnant with me."

I paused for a moment. I felt this burning, almost bubbling, sensation in my chest. The words shot out. "**Liar!** You are such a liar. How could your father have told you the things he did if he died before you were born?" I felt disappointed. It was almost painful to find an undeniable flaw in your story. I realized on some level I had believed you. *At least I wanted to.*

I expected you to shout. Instead, you smiled. Those dimples had some sort of power over me. "He talks to me all the time. He wrote me letters before I was born. I found a bunch of them in the attic a long time ago."

"He wrote you letters?"

"He did. Mom must not have named me what he wanted her to though. All of his letters were addressed to 'My daughter Claire.' "As soon as you spoke, I knew it was a perfect fit. Your name was beautiful, but Claire seemed to capture you, all of you. So fragile, mysterious, strong, and beautiful, all wrapped into a song-like package.

"I still remember the day I found them. It was raining so I went to the attic to find something to do. The letters were all wedged in the third drawer of a dusty dresser, the kind Mom knew I'd find icky. At first, I was so excited. I opened three on the spot. But now I save them. I only open one a year on my birthday. I like to pretend it's my dad sending me a birthday card."

You were standing now. You waved your arms in the wind. Champagne splattered everywhere. It dripped from our faces onto the chairs and wooden floor. I reached to grab your glass before it fell. That's when our fingers touched. Your skin was so warm. As the breeze blew against my now damp shirt, I finally noticed how cold I was.

"3 days, 7 hours, 36 minutes." You said. I realized you were looking at my watch. A small tear was in the corner of your eye. It glimmered in the porch light. "Do you think I'll be lonely?"

This was not the first time you asked me that question. I was adaptable. I could be in a crowd or alone. Either way I was fine. You were *different*. You *needed* someone by your side. It was like if someone didn't acknowledge your existence, you didn't exist. That scared the hell out of you.

I stood up. The wind blew your long hair into my face. The smell of champagne flowed through my veins. We were *alone*. Not just on your porch, but everywhere. You were all I could see, hear, smell, and feel. "I'm not going anywhere," I said.

Our lips met, and I finally got to taste you. I didn't know how much time passed or if you'd remember. For all I knew, we kissed until the sun rose. But it lasted *forever*. No matter the length, our moment was eternal.

We removed our wet shirts and threw them under your humming porch light. They waited there, forever immortalized in the time when we created our own pile of dirty laundry.

Beneath
The Surface

She squinted at the door. Her mind rehearsed what she needed to say. The most difficult part would be containing her smile.

The heavyset man next to her broke the silence. "You're fine taking the reins, aren't you?"

"Of course, I know how to handle him."

"I figured it'd be best this way. He's mostly worked under you." The man rubbed the tip of his balding head. "Just keep it professional. The last thing we need is more bad press."

"It's been a long time coming," the young woman said. She bit her unshaven upper lip to conceal an emerging grin. "The way I see it, this gives us a clear-cut way to be done *with him."*

"That's a positive spin to put on a foreclosure." The *man chuckled to himself and took a sip of coffee.*

I knocked on the door. They turned to face me. The man cleared his throat, "Come in, Conner."

***

I slept on the right side of the bed. I don't know why, but I always did. Perhaps it was muscle memory? Or maybe I just enjoyed staring out the window. It's what I was preoccupying my time with now. With my face half-buried in the soft pillow, I dissected my surroundings. The sun was setting, but still provided enough light to open the outside world to my gaze. I stared across our yard and focused on the old bakery across the street. The red "Open" sign flickered. It was Saturday evening, but it was still full of people. Briefly, I wondered if they were hiring.

My boyfriend sat upright, almost erect, on the left bedside. He was thumbing through one of his magazines with an impish grin.

"Do you really enjoy that?"

Kane turned to me and raised his eyebrow. "Of

course." He stroked his fingers slowly over the thin paper nipple of the featured bottle blond. This was accompanied by a smirk.

Alice told me not to be intimidated by his sexuality, and for the most part I wasn't. There was just something odd about seeing my boyfriend occasionally read Playboy to get in the mood. I once asked him if he needed both men and women to be satisfied. "No," he had said. "I just feel less guilty jerking off to girls." Alice thought it was hilarious. I hadn't wanted to admit it, but I agreed.

Under the covers, I grabbed his leg and pulled him to face me. The magazine fell to the floor (where it belonged). I massaged his thigh, "Do we really have to go?"

He kissed my lips lightly, then placed his hand gently to my face. "Yes," he said while tucking his chin and flashing a perfect smile. *The damn manipulator.* "You're the guest of honor."

"I know, but they'll probably ask about work." As I spoke, I felt hollow in my chest as the air seeped deeper.

"If it comes up, just say you're looking for a new job. It makes sense. You said your boss was a bitch, besides, there are bound to be so many more opportunities for you now."

That didn't mean I'd get any. I looked away from him

and stared up at the ceiling. *Kane probably needs the magazine to stay hard, with the way I'm acting.* "Some of the new employees got to keep their job."

"Conner," I felt Kane's hand on my cheek. He turned me to face him. "If we survived the time you called me Niles, we can survive this." He laughed.

I released his leg so I could pull his hand off my face. "Shut up," I said. He wrapped his hand around my back and guided me closer. I leaned over his ear and whispered, "If you're good, I'll let you call me Carmen and pretend I'm a bottle blond." I imagined he thought it was funny, but he didn't laugh. Instead, he thrust me under him.

For a moment, my thoughts were clear of any lingering notions of work, where to find a new job, or how to explain it all to my friends. For a moment . . .

***

"A toast to Conner, turns out he's smarter than he looks" Ashton said. He and his wife, Monica, sat across from us with their glasses raised. Kane and I extended ours. Several simultaneous "clinks" echoed around the waving liquid. Together, we all took a sip.

"Seriously though," Ashton said after a few extra gulps. His swimmer lungs never failed to amaze me. "Congratulations man, you earned this. But don't think I'm going to start calling you Dr. Mills."

"Oh, stop it," Monica lightly smacked Ashton's shoulder. "He's just jealous because he never finished his PhD."

"Join the club," Kane said raising his glass and engaging in another sip.

"I know, who would've thought out of the three of us, Conner would be the one to finish?" Ashton laughed for a second. He briefly glanced at Monica who was shaking her head with a smirk. "Hell, who am I kidding. I always knew this guy was brilliant; smartest and fastest guy on our team."

Enough is enough, stop with the compliments. "I'm disappointed, Ashton. Half a glass of champagne and you're already drunk and spreading lies. What happened to the great heavyweight?"

"Let me be proud. I feel like I've earned some credit for your molding. I was the one who convinced you to join our swim club." Ashton paused for another sip. "You still find time to swim with all that studying?"

No, I was out of shape and hadn't touched a pool in

three months. "Not as much as I'd like. Kane's kept it up almost every day."

"And yet Conner would still probably kick my ass."

"Oh Conner, before I forget . . ." Monica chimed in. Without fail, she never allowed a conversation to focus too long on swimming. I couldn't blame her, though. A group of swimmers could be very narrow-minded. "I read 'Dirty Laundry' in *The Lyricist*. It was great! Were the characters based on anyone we know?"

"You mean you didn't catch it?" I smiled. "The drinking, daddy issues, and delusions . . . I was practically writing your husband's name." Monica and I chuckled.

"Writer, swimmer, doctor . . ." Ashton turned to Monica and wiggled his thumb at me. "Is there anything this guy can't do?"

Yeah, maintain stable employment.

"You better back off," Kane said. "Remember, I saw him first." They all laughed. Under the table, Kane slipped his hand onto my thigh. It felt like cement, pinning me to the conversation.

After the food arrived, the conversation shifted to the new robot Ashton's firm was developing. "The market's good for robotics right now," Kane said. "The boss man is having us invest everything we have in it. The work is killing us."

"Maybe you should get Conner to help." Ashton laughed. "He'd have the whole thing knocked out in a couple hours."

"I doubt that," I said. "The best thing I could do for them is make sure Kane stayed focused."

"That'd probably be a useful investment." Ashton said. He grinned to himself. "How's the work at your firm, Conner? Are they worshiping you yet?"

Shit. What was I going to say? I had to think of something. I'm sure I'd have to answer this question in job interviews.

"Conner's actually looking for other opportunities," Kane said. "His firm just shut down his entire department. They basically laid everybody off."

My department didn't close and they only laid off a few people. "Yeah," I said. "Wouldn't you know it. I finally get my doctorate and the place goes to Hell."

"Don't worry," Monica said. "I'm sure you'll bounce back."

What did she mean, bounce back? "I'm not worried," I said. I started to feel a familiar twinge in my stomach.

"Excuse me, I need to use the restroom." I pushed my chair back. It moved quickly for a moment, then was abruptly halted. A gasp and rustling of dishes echoed from behind me. I glanced over my shoulder to see I'd backed into our waiter. "Sorry," I said. He smiled briefly and returned to his work. I became thankful we already had our food, otherwise mine would probably come with a side of saliva.

I was thankful no one else was in the restroom. I made my way to the sink. A young man stared at me through the mirror. His eyes were blue and nose was slightly longer than he'd prefer. Barring those resemblances, the man looked nothing like me. Bags were forming under his eyes, and his face was twice as pale as usual. His mouth hung open, creating the illusion of a long face. He was breathing deeply, yet quickly.

With every breath I took, the air seemed to go slightly deeper than possible. It seeped beneath my lungs and spread into a void in my chest. A void seemed to encompass half my stomach, yet it was impossible to fill. Each time I exhaled, my heart would race. It was as if my body sensed danger; keeping the void occupied with air was the only way to prevent it from consuming me. My mind began to spiral. I thought about my bosses sighing in relief as I left. I thought about Ashton and

Kane. I was the one who finished my doctorate, yet they were the ones with steady income.

I splashed my face with cool sink water. I took a moment to stare at my dripping wet reflection. The sight made me chuckle. The laughing guy in the mirror began to look more like me. Like Alice suggested, I started thinking about the water. I closed my eyes and inhaled the thick stench of chlorine. The water cut evenly around me as I soared past everyone else. In the pool, I was in charge. Then I was in the ocean. The chlorine evaporated and was replaced with warm salty air. We were wrestling in the waves. I splashed him, he splashed me back. We were two best friends, alive and well. Then he started to drift away. I tried to chase after him, but my arms were too heavy to fight the current.

"What's up."

I opened my eyes. Ashton entered the bathroom and parked himself at the closest urinal. I grabbed a paper towel and wiped the water from my face. "Just thinking."

"That's dangerous."

"Is that why you've never tried it?"

Ashton shook his hand, then flushed. "Well I wasn't thinking when I picked my first major. Did I ever tell you that I was once a pre-med major?" He approached the sink and started washing his hands. "I did so bad, they made me switch after my first year. I was really upset, but then I realized I was better off doing something else."

I cocked my head. "What do you mean by that?"

"I mean there are plenty of opportunities out there. Probably some that you'll enjoy a Hell of a lot more."

I smiled lightly. "Thanks." Then for some reason, I continued to speak. "You know, my boss was a real bitch. All she said was 'Unfortunately, we'll have to let you go.' I guess that was code for: Thank you for your hard work, sorry to see you go, best of luck, and by the way congrats on your doctorate. I just hate that word; unfortunately. People treat it like a disclaimer to be as rude as possible."

"Well I'd love to keep talking, but UNFOOORTUNATELY, our food is getting cold. So, would you kindly move your ass?" Ashton gestured to the door with a smile. I wadded up my paper towel and threw it at him.

When the check arrived, I instinctively reached for it. Upon remembering I was broke, I paused and hoped Kane would take the hint. But before he even had time to react, Ashton snatched the bill. "This is on us."

"Are you sure," I said. "You don't have to." *But since I*

was broke, he actually did.

"Yeah, it's the least we could do. After all, it's your big day." Kane and I both thanked him. After gathering our belongings and exchanging hugs with our dinner guests, we made our way to the door.

After we left, Monica turned to her husband. "You could have at least let them leave the tip."

"We should help them," Ashton said. "They're going to need it. Conner just got sacked."

"Poor guy. He was trying so hard to pretend like it wasn't bothering him."

"Yeah, I caught him crying in the bathroom. I think he was talking to himself or something before I came in. Then he started bitching about his old boss."

"No one will hire him if he continues to blame others." Monica shrugged her shoulders and sighed. "I guess they'll give doctorates to anyone nowadays."

"No, the guy is book smart. He's a great student, he just doesn't know how to handle himself in actual life." Ashton threw down his credit card and waited for the waiter.

***

Dr. Alice was a slim woman of about five and a half feet. She was equipped with her trademark rectangular glasses and business attire. Her only feature that wasn't professional was the tattoo beginning on her right wrist. It was blue and wavy, almost like a cloud or butterfly's wing. I'd never seen the entire picture. *Perhaps it went all the way up her arm? Maybe further?*

After a firm handshake, I sat and we began talking. She asked about Kane and I asked about her husband. "Dave's doing well. He's on a business trip in Atlanta," she said. As usual, our sessions began with light conversation.

The desk next to me had a few new objects. Besides the typical stress ball, slinky, and silly putty, there was now a foam handball and fidget spinner. Normally, I went with the slinky, but decided to give the spinner a try. I pinched it between my pointer finger and thumb, and twirled.

"These things came out of nowhere, I feel like everyone has one now."

"There're a hit in this office. All the cool doctors have them."

"I guess I should get one."

She smiled. "Does this mean you finished the degree?" We talked about our courses and thesis presentations, and the difficulty of doing it amongst life's commitments. We laughed, saying we both liked being called doctor, but didn't want anyone to know it. Alice agreed that having a doctorate didn't make her feel any smarter. Half the time, I felt like an imposter hiding behind it.

"Did you find any time to write while you were finishing classes?" She asked after a brief silence.

"Yes," I sat up eagerly. "My latest story was actually published in a local magazine."

"That's wonderful. Is it one I'm familiar with?"

I slumped back in my seat, uncomfortable for the first time since the session started. "No, I don't think you are." I stopped twirling the spinner and placed it on the table. "I guess it's been a while since we've talked."

"That just means we have a lot to catch up on." She adjusted her glasses and glanced down at her clipboard. "Have you still been swimming?"

"Some, not as much since I started working." I scuffed. "I guess I'll have more time now." I laughed cautiously.

"Do you want to talk about work?"

"There's not much to talk about. My bosses weren't happy with the work I was doing, so they got rid of me."

"On the phone, you said you were let go. Weren't there others who were let go as well?"

I glanced around the room, searching for anything other than her eyes. "They were happy to see me go. There were others who hadn't been there as long as me, who got to keep their jobs."

"I see." I wasn't looking at her, but I imagined she was still sitting perfectly erect with her hands neatly folded over her clipboard. "Conner, do you remember what we talked about in our last session?"

"Yep," I reached into my pocket and placed the bottle on the table with a little more force than intended. The container rattled as the pills raced back to the bottom. My gaze returned to her face. I was almost disappointed that her expression didn't change. There was no twitch, no look of guilt, not even a question of why I still had them despite my previous objections.

"Have you been taking them?"

"No, I know you think I need them . . ."

She raised her hand, holding her pointer finger up. This was our established code for when either of us had an important point to make while the other was still talking. Basically, a way to say, 'shut the fuck up,' politely. I obeyed.

"I never said you needed the pills, Conner. We only insist upon them in extreme cases, and even then, it's only a recommendation. What I prescribed is a low dose and was meant only as a tool to be used at your discretion. I apologize if I offended you during our last session, my intent was not to be forceful."

Of course, it was offensive! "You didn't offend me."

"I know there's a stereotype associated with taking medication, much like seeing a counselor. But as you pointed out in our previous sessions, seeking a little assistance doesn't mean something is wrong with you. It's daunting to think that a tiny pill bottle is going to influence your behavior."

Like she would know.

"I've been on antidepressants for several years."

Or maybe she would. "I'm sorry." Those weren't the right words to say, but she smiled indicating she knew what I meant. "So, you don't think I'm an extreme case."

"No," she laughed a little to herself. "The people we worry about are the ones who are a danger to others or themselves. I don't think that's you."

It flashed before me so suddenly; the moist sand, salty air, water in my lungs . . . and the darkness. Then Kane, standing over me, dripping wet. He had been angry, and I had been numb. It was the one thing I never told Alice.

"Do you really think these pills could be good for me?"

"Only you can answer that. They may help reduce some of the sensations you say you've experienced, or they may not. I find some patients like having a little additional stress, they say it keeps them productive. What I want you to do is take a few days to really think about how you've been feeling lately. If you do that, the answer should become clear."

She stood up and extended her hand. This was another established code meaning, 'our time is up, get the hell out of my office.' "I hope you come see me again soon, Conner." She released my hand and looked briefly at her clipboard. "Oh, and do send me a copy of your latest story."

***

When I returned home, I was greeted by the lurid sound of cheers behind a boisterous announcer. "That was truly a historic catch, ladies and gentlemen! Let's see what the ref says . . . And we have a touchdown!"

The ringing in my ears, coupled with my superior detective skills, concluded that Kane was watching a football game.

"Kane," I called out. No answer. I followed the commotion to our living room. Kane was sitting on the edge of the couch, cheering at the TV. "Kane," I repeated at the top of my lungs.

He took notice of me. I assumed he said, "Hello," but that was solely based on my lip-reading abilities. He reached for the remote and lowered the volume.

"There you are," he said. "I've been home for like an hour. Where have you been?"

"Just running some errands."

"Really, I would've thought you'd be taking advantage of the free time. If I were you, I would've been here with my legs propped up."

I averted my gaze to the television. "Are we winning?"

"Yeah, game just ended." *Explains why he was willing to lower the volume.* He sprang to his feet. "I have an idea. Why don't we go swimming?"

Swimming sounded fantastic, but as soon as he spoke the words, my chest began to twitch. *Was I nervous about swimming with him?* I swam varsity, I was great. I'd just been out of the water of awhile, and Kane had been training. *Why should that matter?* My stomach twitched again.

"That sounds relaxing. I'd love to."

***

The smell of chlorine seemed foreign to me. I recognized it, but had forgotten so many of the details . . . How it was so pungent that it felt like inhaling mist or how the odor lingered in the roof of your mouth, almost tickling the inside of your nose.

Kane advanced to the edge of the pool. His toned arms and six-pack were still easily visible from a distance. If a stranger were to look at us, they wouldn't assume I was the one who swam varsity.

"I hate this part." Kane said. "Plunging into the cold water is the worst."

"I know. In college I always made one of my teammates push me in." I said with a slight smile. "I can always do the same for you."

"I've got a better idea. Let's race." He tried to sound spontaneous, but it's difficult to believe the notion just then crept into his mind.

"I don't know. It's been awhile. I think I need to warm up first."

"This will be our warm-up. We'll just race down and back. If we're moving fast, it won't feel as cold."

"I really don't want to."

"It's such a short race. I promise it'll feel good."

I moved to the lane next to him and applied my goggles and cap. Kane was jumping and stretching his arms with short dynamic movements. It was a common technique for swimmers to warm-up before a big competition.

"I thought this race was our warm up."

"The water's cold, man. Unfortunately, I have to do something to brace myself."

I slightly nodded, then pressed my goggles tighter into my face. On the count of three, Kane and I dove into the shrieking, chlorinated water.

Unfortunately, God I hated that word. My arms felt stiff, like they were slapping the water. When I was in shape, they smoothly glided. *Man, I was out of shape.* I realized my head was up. I needed to keep it down. That was proper technique. *UNFOOORTUNATELY, this didn't feel good! What did he even mean by that? It's unfortunate when you regret something, not when you need to stretch, or fire someone you hate.* I approached the wall. *Focus.* I flip-turned and pushed off with my legs. *My legs were so heavy. Don't think, focus.* A figure was in the corner of my eye. It was probably Kane. *Was he ahead of me? Of course, he was ahead of me. Don't give up. Race him!* I closed my eyes. My arms pulled harder. Legs kicked faster. *The wall was my goal. Nothing else mattered. Not my writing, not my doctorate, not my unemployment. The wall. The wall was everything.*

My hand collided with the firm surface. Immediately, my head jerked to the side. Panting to catch my breath, I saw Kane resting on the wall, clearly waiting on me. He was smiling.

Kane extended his hand. I tried to pretend like I didn't see it. Like I was busy catching my breath or looking at something in the gutter. "Nice swim," he said.

I turned to him, smiled. Limply, I took his hand. "It wasn't really, but thanks."

"Let's keep moving. You've got to do something to shake that rust off." Kane laughed before submerging and pushing off the wall.

I stared at my arms. They felt numb. I scrunched my face at the traitors. Perhaps it was my panting, maybe it was being in the water again . . . but I thought of that night on the beach. The roaring of the waves, salt water in my lungs, Kane standing over me . . . *Kane! I told him I didn't want to race.*

I imagined Kane's face. My fist clenched. My bosses came next. First, fat and balding. Next, female and mustached. Then I thought of Alice's face, then Ashton's and Monica's . . . I don't know which face I was thinking about when I struck my own.

***

I waited a few minutes before joining Kane in the locker room showers. The only noise I could hear was from his solitary shower. Since we were alone, I stripped off all my clothes.

"You had a good swim." I spoke while turning on my shower. I immediately started washing my hair, but it was pointless. I could still hear him.

"I knew I'd get you sooner or later," He said with a boyish grin I normally found attractive. "I guess, for once, you're buying me the victory dinner."

"Well I'd love to, but I'm unemployed and don't have any money."

"Conner, don't start this again." He stepped out of the falling water, towards me. He was completely naked except for a streak of soap bubbles down his chest. "You'll get a job soon and the only reason I beat you is because I've been training. Just practice some more, and you'll get back in shape."

"Because it's that easy, isn't it?" I cast Kane a glare that matched my sarcastic tone. Then I realized I had left the shower and was standing only a few inches from him.

"God Conner, you're acting like the world's ending because one job didn't work out. How many times do I need to say that you'll find another job? You have a fucking doctorate."

"I know I have a doctorate! I have one and . . ." I trailed off. My volume lowered and speech slowed. ". . .and I haven't even savored it. I accomplished something so few people do, and I haven't even allowed myself to be happy about it."

We were both quiet. The only sound came from the water splattering against the tiled floor. "Hey, it's fine," Kane finally said. "You're just getting over a lot of stress. It's normal to be a bit emotional."

"Kane," I said. My voice was softer and slower than before. "I think something's wrong with me. I might have anxiety or something. Alice thinks . . ."

"I thought you stopped seeing her."

"I did for a while, but I went back this morning."

"Conner, she wants to convince you that you've got issues, so you'll keep coming to her. You said it yourself, she tried to force drugs on you."

"She prescribed some mild pills, so I'd have them if I wanted. She said I didn't need them because I'm not a danger to myself, but she doesn't know . . ."

"Doesn't know what?" His voice sounded concerned, but I spoke as if it hadn't.

"Doesn't know I went into the ocean and let myself sink; that you had to save me." My eyes were closed, and hands were shaking.

"Conner," his voice sounded closer. I felt his hand on my shoulder; it moved down my arm slowly. "That was years ago. Your best friend had just died." He smiled, giving himself more time to think of other explanations. "Besides, you weren't going to let yourself drown. You said you wanted to go under the water to think. It makes sense. It was just dark, and I didn't realize what you were doing; that's why I pulled you out."

"If it was no big deal, why did you recommend I see a counselor?"

He removed his hand from my arm and gestured with

it. "Because your friend died. It was a traumatic event. We've all experienced them, and all needed someone to talk to. I just don't want someone making you think you have a mental disorder because you react to a few stressful situations."

He looked so genuine, the same way he looked that night on the beach. It wasn't that he didn't want to understand, it was that he couldn't. "I'll see you later." Without turning off my water, I left the showers and entered the adjacent changing room. Quickly, I patted myself dry with a towel.

"Where are you going?" I heard him turn off both showers. He entered the changing room, dripping wet and soap-covered.

"I just need a couple hours. I'll see you at home tonight." I thrust my head through my shirt hole, grabbed my bag, and made my way to the exit.

The door slammed behind me, igniting a vibrant echo. When the sound cleared, my boyfriend was left alone. Slowly, he took a towel and dried himself. Meticulously, he removed every drop from his body. When he was finished, he secured the towel around his waist and removed a phone from his bag. He tapped a few buttons and placed it to his ear.

"Hey, it's me. He's in panic mode again." He said.

He was silent for a moment.

"I know. I do love him," he said. "I just don't know how much more of this I can take."

***

The fleeting sunlight glistened off the lakefront. A breeze enabled some miniature waves to crash upon the sandy shore. I walked along the sand and rocks and imagined I was on a beach at sunset. But when I closed my eyes, I knew where I really was. The smell gave it away. The sand, water, even the waves could be replicated, but not the salty air.

Though not a beach, the landscape was beautiful. The climax of my newly-published story took place on a porch. *Maybe it would have been better by the lake. The lake, appearing to be an ocean, could represent the girl's relationship with her father.* My bare feet dragged through the damp sand and entered the cool lake water. A jarring and refreshing coldness shivered up my legs. *Maybe the girls could even go for a brief swim . . .* A small wave crashed against my feet and soaked the bottom of my pants leg. I glanced down; the water dimly reflected my face. I realized I was smiling.

I turned from the water and looked towards the sky.

These thoughts were pointless, the story was already published. Besides, I didn't have time to work on a story, not while I was unemployed. I left the water and sat in the sand.

While noticing how the sand beads stuck to my wet feet, I decided to check my phone. Two missed calls from Kane. I opened the portable device and drafted words 'Hey. How are you?' I reread the message three times before finally pressing "Send."

Her response was almost instant, 'Hello Conner. Is everything alright?'

Of course Alice would ask that. I wouldn't be messaging her if everything was fine. 'Yes, I'm good,' I responded.

'Ok. I'm here if you need to talk.'

I typed the words 'Thank you!' Then, almost as if by reflex, I deleted the text and hit the call button.

"Hello Conner. How are you doing?" Her voice sounded neither annoyed nor concerned.

I wanted to tell her about the argument; about my reaction to Kane beating me. Instead, I said "Can someone be a happy person if they're constantly stressed? Like they enjoy doing lots of things, but sometimes worry too much about . . . everything."

"It's certainly more difficult. It's important to balance stressful situations with pleasant thoughts. Remember when we talked about envisioning something happy?"

I closed my eyes and listened to the waves crash upon one another. For an instant, I thought I smelled salt in the air. "Alice, what if the place you think about no longer makes you happy?"

"You just have to find another. Also, you don't have to think of a place. Your happy thought could be an accomplishment, idea, or even a moment in time. Just make sure you can focus on what it is that makes you feel that happiness. Then see if you can apply your findings to the stressful situation."

We were silent for a while. She stayed on the line. I pressed the phone tight against my ear and listened to her hushed breath cycles.

I looked again at the lake. It was getting dark now. The wind was blowing lightly but continuously. It reminded me of the night Kane pulled me from the ocean. Finally, I spoke. "Alice, why is this so hard?"

"Sometimes people have trouble accepting that they're imperfect humans. They treat their shortcomings like cancer. If they let it spread, it consumes everything."

I thanked Alice for her time. Before hanging up, I promised to send her a copy of 'Dirty Laundry,' after I made a few revisions. I stood up and lightly patted the sand from my pants; I knew what I had to do.

Before leaving the 'beach,' I picked up a rock and tossed it into the water. It sank without a single skip. Alice said anxiety was closely linked to depression. In my mind, I knew I wouldn't have gone through with it. But, my mind had been unreliable lately.

***

My car screeched to a halt before the large house. Once my door was open, my nostrils were struck with the familiar scent of freshly chopped grass. The driveway was illuminated with multiple, evenly spaced, solar powered outdoor torches.

The doorbell emitted a nostalgic chime which was slightly muffled by the house walls. I pushed it twice before hearing feet shuffle behind the doorframe. The door was opened half a minute later, allowing the home owner enough time to peer through the peephole.

"Hey Conner!" My mother ushered me inside and

encased me in a hug.

I greeted her warmly before proceeding to our living room. Dad was away on a business trip. *I had my chance.*

Once Mom was settled into a seat across from me, she began speaking. "This is a surprise. Is everything alright?" She briefly paused for a breath. "How are things at the firm?"

"I was let go."

"What?" She sat up instantly. The bottom half of her lip retreated into her mouth, giving her something to bite. "How could that happen?"

"It doesn't matter. Mom, I need . . ."

"Did they give you a reason? They must have said something . . ."

"Why didn't you tell me about your cancer?"

"What?" Mom retreated into her chair. Her bottom lip was now free, her mouth slightly ajar.

"Years ago, when you were diagnosed with breast cancer, you hid it from me. I want to know why." The sea-like circulation of the house's heating system contorted into the screeching hum of the bathroom ceiling fan. The dog's paws sprang to life and clicked across the floor. Mother sat before me, exposed.

"Sweetie, I didn't tell anyone. It was my business."

The temperament of her answer led me to believe she misunderstood the nature of my question. "I'm not mad. I just want to know."

"Why are we talking about this? It was years ago."

The screeching flooded the room with enough force to send a wolf fleeing in terror. *She had to have it on. There was no other explanation.* "I need to know, Mom. I need to know why you couldn't admit you were suffering."

A full head of hair shielded Mom's barren face. "I just love chocolate." She parsed her lips as if holding the taste on the tip of her tongue. "But I restrict myself. I have two pieces of chocolate cake a year; birthday and Christmas. I exercise five times a week. I put so much effort into living a healthy life . . . Then suddenly I'm sick. I'm told I may not live, while people who never even considered their health are fine. For the first time, I looked at my body with pity and doubt. I couldn't let you look at me like that."

***

A single light radiated from our living room window. Kane was an all-or-nothing kind of guy. If he was awake, the house would've been a miniature Times Square in terms of light. *Maybe he forgot to turn it off when he went to bed?*

I entered the house quietly. I decided to turn off the light before slipping into bed. Nights like tonight made me wish we had a guest room. *I hope Kane is asleep.*

To my surprise, Kane was awake. He was sitting in the living room, looking at a couple of books amidst a solitary lamp. "Hey," he said. I was relieved when he didn't question where I had been or yell at me for how I behaved.

I recognized the book next to him. It was *The Lyricist*, where my story was published. The book clenched in his lap was a different story. It was large, hard-backed item with a dark-red leather covering that had some sort of cursive engraving.

"What are you looking at?"

"I re-read your story. It's really good." He noticed my eyes were fixated on his lap. "This." He held up the red leather. "This, is a scrap book. It's of us." As soon as he spoke, I noticed the cursive engraving were our initials.

"You have so much going for you," he said. "I know you've had some shit with your work, but that seemed so small." He glanced down at the scrap book. "You always seemed happy."

"I have a good life and I'm a happy person . . ." I

paused briefly, ". . .until I'm not. Things will be going great and then something will happen. Suddenly, my best friend is dead, or I get feelings for someone who doesn't love me back, or I'm laid off from a job I thought was going well. Then everything just spirals out of control."

I knew what he was going to say, but I couldn't give him the chance. I avoided his eyes and continued. "I know those things would mess with anyone, but I don't think it's the same with me. I . . . I get nervous. Suddenly, everything I do is wrong. There's this feeling, this sensation, in my chest. Then I start to imagine things."

"What kind of things?" His voice sounded calm, but had a questioning tone.

"Don't worry, nothing supernatural or out of the ordinary." I sighed and almost laughed. "That's actually the problem. The things I imagine seem real. I know they're not, or at least might not be. But I'll think about stuff like my bosses being happy to let me go, my friends belittling me, even you wanting to leave me. I'll replay these thoughts over and over again. The images will become more vivid; people's words clearer." I held my hands together. My fingers started to twitch. I spoke more softly.

"I'll do this until they seem like they actually

happened."

I looked back at Kane. He maintained eye contact until I was finished. "Conner, did these fears and sensations stop you from pursuing a writing career?"

I didn't have an answer.

"If you think you need the pills, you should take them. And if Alice helps you, then you should see her." He exhaled slowly. "Just don't let this define you. You're more than a mental disorder."

I smiled. "I guess if we could deal with the time you made me race you in a freezing-ass pool, we can deal with this."

He smirked and held up the leather binding. "I made this for your birthday. Want a sneak peek?"

I sat next to him, and turned the page. Images from my life stretched before me. One picture depicted Kane and me moving into our house. We were in the living room pretending to engage in a tug-of-war battle over the TV. It had been a bright day; sunlight was visible through the window frame. Another showed me at a Halloween party. I was shirtless, with my legs encased in a large tailfin suit. Party-goers constantly referred to me as a mermaid, I had to correct them and say I was a merman. I remembered not being able to walk in the costume and having to convince people to carry me from room to room. Then I came across a picture of me in a graduation cap and a brightly colored robe with three velvet bands on each arm. I was with Kane and my family at an ice cream shop. The store owner had given us all complementary scoops. I'd almost forgotten about that.

"Mom took this picture three weeks ago."

"Your parents helped me with this. There're several blank pages in the back. I figured we could keep filling them together."

"Thank you." They were two simple words, but I didn't know how else to express my gratitude. He'd literally given me a book of happy memories.

"Don't thank me yet. You haven't seen the childhood pictures I put in front."

"Oh God, now I'm scared." I commenced flipping towards the front of the book, but a few pages in something caught my eye. A pair of seemingly happy eyes stared back at me. The photograph showed me standing between Kane and Ashton; the salty water and sandy shore behind us.

It was the night I went into the ocean to think. Perhaps my heart had beaten rapidly, perhaps not at all? I had felt so hollow, the night breeze seemed to circulate through my whole body. Kane may have pulled me from the water, but I was still sinking.

Then Kane and I had shared our first kiss. In that moment, the air had rushed back into my lungs. I swam a thousand miles as the world began and ended.

If only for a moment.

About the Author

Andrew McCollister was born in North Carolina to Rick McCollister and Kathey Teague-McCollister. From a young age, Andrew loved exercising his creativity. He and his father often took turns inventing and exchanging stories during rides to school. Later, Andrew attended Catawba College where he majored in writing and graduated Magna Cum Laude with College Honors. After that, he traveled to

Boston where he earned his MBA and Masters in the Science of Accounting from Northeastern University.

Andrew currently lives in Cleveland, Ohio. There he works, and amazingly enough, enjoys the profession of accounting at Zuber Gardner CPA's. When he's not crunching the numbers or delving into fiction, Andrew is spending time in the pool. He is a nationally ranked swimmer who started training the age of six.

Andrew is featured in numerous publications, including "North Carolina's Best Emerging Poets." However, one of his greatest dreams has been to publish a book. Andrew couldn't be prouder of his first novel "Beneath the Surface" and of the friends and family who have supported him along the way.

Made in the USA
Lexington, KY
15 March 2018